CORPORATE LAWBREAKING AND INTERACTIVE COMPLIANCE

CORPORATE LAWBREAKING AND INTERACTIVE COMPLIANCE

Resolving the Regulation-Deregulation Dichotomy

Edited by
JAY A. SIGLER and
JOSEPH E. MURPHY
Foreword by JOHN BRAITHWAITE

Q
QUORUM BOOKS
New York • Westport, Connecticut • London

Library of Congress Cataloging-in-Publication Data

Corporate lawbreaking and interactive compliance : resolving the regulation-deregulation dichotomy / edited by Jay A. Sigler and Joseph E. Murphy ; foreword by John Braithwaite.
p. cm.
Includes bibliographical references and index.
ISBN 0-89930-490-7 (alk. paper)
1. Corporation law—United States. 2. Corporation law—United States—Criminal provisions. 3. Trade regulation—United States. 4. Industry and state—United States. 5. Industry—Social aspects—United States. I. Sigler, Jay A. II. Murphy, Joseph E.
KF1414.C66 1991
346.73'066—dc20 90-26209
[347.30666]

British Library Cataloguing in Publication Data is available.

Library of Congress Catalog Card Number: 90-26209
ISBN: 0-89930-490-7

First published in 1991

Quorum Books, 88 Post Road West, Westport, CT 06881
An imprint of Greenwood Publishing Group, Inc.

Printed in the United States of America

The paper used in this book complies with the Permanent Paper Standard issued by the National Information Standards Organization (Z39.48–1984).

10 9 8 7 6 5 4 3 2 1

Copyright Acknowledgments

Excerpts from "Minimizing Corporate Civil and Criminal Liability: A Second Look at Corporate Codes of Conduct," by Harvey L. Pitt and Karl A. Groskaufmanis is reprinted with permission of publisher, © 1990 The Georgetown Law Journal Association.

To our families and to our new-found colleagues who share our quest for interactive corporate compliance

Contents

Foreword

John Braithwaite

Jay A. Sigler and Joseph E. Murphy's *Interactive Corporate Compliance* was one of the most important books on American business to be published in the 1980s. A challenge for the 1990s is to show how the policy in that book can be put into practice. This is the challenge that the present volume seeks to meet.

Interactive corporate compliance is about encouraging the establishment of reliable self-regulatory systems within corporations. Sigler and Murphy propose a kind of social contract between business and government—one in which government scrutiny is reduced in return for self-regulatory vigilance. It is a proposal to move beyond the barren dichotomy between regulation and deregulation. Regulation can involve excessive rigidity and cost, while the deregulation of the Reagan era conduced to both excess and political reversal. Fresh approaches are needed that foster both cooperation and dynamism in the relationship between business and government.

Even though such fresh approaches are not being pursued on a wide scale in the United States, the contributions in this book show that they are possible. It shows that in a decentralized political system, such as that in the United States, with multiple sources of power, regulatory innovations can get a foothold and be tested out in locales as unlikely as Camden County, New Jersey.

It seems to me that interactive corporate compliance is different from other attempts to encourage self-regulation in that it is not grounded in unrealistically rosy expectations about the ethics of the business community. It is, after all, an interactive policy program. If business is reckless and irresponsible, and it can often be, then the privilege of reduced government intervention is revoked.

New York Attorney General Robert Abrams recognizes this in his chapter when he calls for "a partnership between government and business, based on a foundation of enforcement." He illustrates such a partnership through the initiatives his administration has taken to foster in-house audits by firms that work with toxic chemicals. Attorney General Abrams envisages a three-part strategy for corporate compliance: continued strong government enforcement, a new emphasis on government-corporate partnerships for preventive action, and the emergence of citizen action as a prod for ethical corporate conduct.

This is unexceptionable. It raises, however, the fundamental question of how to develop a practical policy that prevents the different parts of this strategy from undermining each other. How do we ensure that citizen activism does not result in demands for enforcement that fail to be interactive—for example, demands for tough criminal enforcement against a company that is unlucky enough to suffer a toxic chemical spill after it has put in place the best possible in-house auditing programs, the best possible technology, and the most good faith staff training programs conceivable? And when this happens, how can one sustain a government-corporate partnership for preventive action?

I suspect that the answer to this dilemma is to more fully include citizen groups in the partnership. Then citizen groups will be in a better position to know the cases where tough enforcement is called for (because the firm has acted in bad faith) and to recognize the cases where good faith efforts warrant a different kind of response. It is rational for citizen groups to demand relentless (noninteractive) punishment against corporate offenders so long as these citizen groups are kept information-poor, powerless, and away from the negotiating table when the guidelines for interactive compliance are worked out.

Interactive corporate compliance will never be a practical program unless it can inspire confidence in citizen groups as well as in the business community. It will be a politically dangerous program so long as it gives wide discretion to regulators to grant immunity from law enforcement without putting in place some community checks and balances against the abuse of that discretion. The challenge, therefore, is in the detail of how to design policies that keep the three elements of the Abrams strategy in creative tension.

Harvey L. Pitt and Karl A. Groskaufmanis enter very directly into the spirit of interactive corporate compliance. Their main contribution is to suggest a new legal standard to reward corporate due diligence in implementing corporate codes of conduct. If the corporation passes the tests of due diligence that are proposed, Pitt and Groskaufmanis suggest that this should be taken into account in private tort actions and should be a defense in certain administrative and criminal actions. In assessing due diligence, the burden should lie with the corporation to prove that it had an effective compliance program. This done, the court should evaluate the integrity of the corporation's commitment to internal compliance by taking account of the length of time the code has been in operation, whether it has been adopted with active involvement of the board of directors, the scope and specificity of the code, its clarity, the vigor with which it is communicated to employees, the monitoring of compliance, the integration of the code into corporate culture, and evidence of its enforcement.

Jay A. Sigler describes a variety of experiments with interactive corporate compliance from around the United States, and, for his part, Louis S. Bezich gives a detailed account of a single experiment in implementation—the regulation of health standards for restaurants in Camden County, New Jersey. The Camden County program aims to provide a win-win outcome to the regulatory game by (1) motivating restaurants to exceed minimum inspection standards with a positive incentive—the Silver Platter Award—and (2) increasing compliance and reducing enforcement costs for county government. When restaurants voluntarily enroll in the program, they must send at least one employee each year to a county-administered food service training class and conduct quarterly self-inspections according to a mandated format. In return, they are exempted from government inspections.

Bezich gives a valuable account of how the different stakeholders in this regulatory arena were persuaded of the value of the program. A key omission in this discussion is what the response will be when a serious outbreak of food-borne illness is caused by a restaurant holding a Silver Platter Award. Unless interactive compliance programs are designed so that they can handle such disasters, they will not survive. Such design, it seems to me, requires open discussion of the possibility that this will occur with all interest groups at the time the program is sold. This is the starting point for a consensus among the interest groups as to what should happen when it does occur.

Then, when the unthinkable happens, the program will not collapse. Rather, the interest groups will all understand that it was in the cards that one day this would occur. Far from being thrown into a political panic, they will have an agreed position on what will be done to the Silver Platter Award restaurant that caused the outbreak. Carefully crafted press releases will be ready to persuade the community that the outbreak does not call into question the integrity of the program; rather, it calls into question the integrity of the management, staff, or owners of a particular restaurant. Only if industry associations stand ready to join in the public condemnation of the guilty actors and if political leaders and consumer groups stand ready to publicly support the program can the program survive such a disaster.

Paul M. Carren and Richard B. Pazornik document corporate self-enforcement programs from the point of view of a major American professional accounting firm. It is interesting to note that corporate compliance is being given serious attention by firms that have earned a reputation for reliability in financial matters. The authors show why a corporate ethics policy is necessary, discuss what it should contain, and explain who should implement it and how.

In his chapter, Joseph E. Murphy gives practical advice to corporate counsel regarding what they can do to make an interactive corporate compliance program work. This advice is grounded in Murphy's own rich experience as a senior counsel of a large corporation. He fills out the detail of three basic axioms: (1) Get senior management actively involved, (2) use results-oriented education and awareness programs, and (3) make compliance part of management's system of incentives and controls.

Jeffrey M. Kaplan describes an interesting Scared Straight program directed not so much at the masterminds of corporate crimes, but at their helpers, the middle managers. This New York program is run by the Business Ethics Study Team (BEST). Its motivational focus is on what happens to middle managers during the crucial ten seconds when their boss asks, and then demands, that they sign off on an illegality. How can one give middle managers the strength to "just say no" when the boss insists that he or she will not leave without the signature? The innovative answer of the BEST program is to scare them straight through educational programs that confront them with middle managers who said yes and ended up as the scapegoats who went to prison for the crime. The anecdotal feedback reported by Kaplan suggests that the program forces at least some executives to confront the shame it would cause them and their family should they be convicted of a corporate criminal offense.

The chapters by Thomas L. Shaffer and W. Richard Sherman deal with the education of young entrants into law and corporate business, respectively. They show the failure of law schools and business schools to develop the kinds of cooperative dispositions essential to the success of interactive corporate compliance. I do not take the import of these critiques to be that law and business schools should replace the sharpening of competitive skills with socialization in cooperative skills. There is no reason why both cannot be done; in the personality structures of effective, responsible human beings there must be places for both cooperation and competition. My observations of the elite of the Australian business community—from the years I served with them as a member of our Economic Planning Advisory Council and from my years serving with our national antitrust agency—indicate that people who are very successful at business are both good at competing and good at cooperating. In the business community—and in law, too, I suspect—competitive skills and coopertive skills are not negatively, but positively, correlated. To succeed in most walks of life—whether business, law, or basketball—we need to be good at both. Perhaps the life of a university professor is one of those exceptions where it matters little if one is an incompetent cooperator. The problem may then be the professors whom we trust to educate our young people in law and business schools. If so, the works of Shaffer and Sherman, and this book generally, may be a start toward persuading academia that the simplistic model of the outside world as endless competition between irreconcilable interests could occasionally be wide of the mark.

John T. Scholz's chapter is important in that it supplies the most sophisticated rationale in the book as to why interactive corporate compliance is desirable. He provides some theoretical insight into why flexible, negotiated compliance can deliver better compliance outcomes to the community at lower cost to industry. Scholz also sees as vital, mechanisms for public accountability for the wide discretion and flexibility granted to regulators when cooperative regulatory enforcement is implemented. However, Scholz is somewhat pessimistic about citizen groups' supporting cooperative regulation, even when it is rational for them to do so in terms of maximizing the regulatory outcomes they seek. This is because citizen groups face an incentive structure driven by the fact that "espousing cooperation is less likely to increase lobbying funds than attacking the opposition."

The implication of this concern is that regulatory scholarship must remedy the neglect of the incentives facing community groups. The literature is rich with analyses of the incentives of business executives and bureaucrats, but poor in analyses of the incentives facing community groups that have considerable influence in shaping the regulatory agenda. If Scholz is right that citizen groups often undermine achievement of their espoused objectives in order to secure a flow of funds, then we need to understand what we can do about the interest that all players of the regulatory game have in changing such a situation.

In countries with a more corporatist style of government than that in the United States, a partial solution lies in unifying all major consumer, environmental, and worker groups under the umbrella of peak councils. The peak council steps in when a member organization seeks notoriety to attract short-term support by undermining the long-term benefits of interactive corporate compliance. The peak council will then mobilize other member organizations (which value the long-term benefits of cooperative, participatory problem solving) to put pressure on the organization seeking to free ride on the cooperation of others by cashing in on an opportunity to be adversative. We see this clearly in Australia, for example, with the way the Australian Council of Trade Unions disciplines member unions that seek to enter into gladiatorial battles with employers to breach agreed national wage-fixing guidelines.

Not only do encompassing organizations have an incentive to discipline free riders (Olson 1965), but also they have a different incentive structure when they are peak councils funded by grants from the central government. In Australia and many other countries, governments have encouraged the empowerment of citizen groups by enabling them to speak with a unified voice in national forums. They have fostered this empowerment by directly funding peak councils such as the Australian Federation of Consumer Organizations, the Australian Conservation Foundation, and the Australian Council on the Rehabilitation of the Disabled.

One cannot simply transplant solutions to these kinds of problems from one country to another. However, the American debate on the role of citizen groups in regulatory enforcement does suffer from a limited imagination as to ways in which the incentive structures confronting citizen groups might be transformed to make them both more powerful and more cooperative. This issue should be given higher priority in the research agenda on how to practice interactive corporate compliance.

This book is an important contribution to the literature sharing experiences we have had in different jurisdictions in struggling to make interactive corporate compliance work. Scholz's suggestion for a National Academy of Regulatory Enforcement would be an exciting way of moving forward from this point.

There is, however, most assuredly a long way to go. The practical steps being taken in the United States today toward interactive corporate compliance are very small. Consider, for example, the U.S. Sentencing Commission's 1989 draft guidelines on the sentencing of corporations. Against the backdrop of fines that are far too low to provide the enforcement that Attorney General Abrams advocated, the commission proposes a sentence discount of only 20 percent for corporations that have credible internal compliance systems. A step in the right direction perhaps, but hardly a big enough step to put in place an incentive structure that will herald a new era of interactive corporate compliance.

The philosophy behind this book is in a sense not to wait for the top-down incentives needed to transform the United States' regulatory culture. Rather, it is to work with examples from the periphery of American polity—such as the regulation of the Camden County restaurant industry—to show those at the center that better regulatory models can be constructed. Toward achieving this aspiration, this book has made an invaluable beginning.

CORPORATE LAWBREAKING AND INTERACTIVE COMPLIANCE

1

A Novel Approach to Business-Government Relationships

Jay A. Sigler and Joseph E. Murphy

In 1988 the Sigler-Murphy book *Interactive Corporate Compliance* was published to provide a fresh look at the topic of governmental regulation and deregulation of business. In the book's subtitle the authors intended to emphasize that there was a workable "alternative to regulatory compulsion." Fortunately, many of the reviewers who read and analyzed the book agreed that it provided a new and provocative approach to one of the central problems of business-government relationships in modern America. However, because more specific examples and more detailed cases were needed to guide business leaders and government officials, this second book builds on the first by giving prominent figures an opportunity to share their perspectives on the possibilities to be found in interactive compliance.

Many groups and individuals are interested in exploring the current meaning and scope of cooperative approaches to corporate compliance. On April 21, 1990, some of the most concerned people were brought together for a conference at New York University's Leonard Stern School of Business. The conference, held under the auspices of the Samuel and May Rudin Foundation, the Stern School, and the Business Ethics Study Team, Inc., was a major event in the spread and elaboration of the ideas originally presented in the 1988 book. These ideas are gathered here for the first time, along with the observations and experiences gained by Joseph E. Murphy and Jay A. Sigler in the intervening years.

In 1988 we traced the rise of the modern American administrative state from 1900 until the election of Ronald Reagan in 1980. We showed that the rise of the administrative state was a response to very real dangers to the health and safety of the people and the financial stability of the economic system. Fear of the power of the great business "trusts" was coupled with a need to intervene in the marketplace to provide safer drugs and more sanitary food. Distrust of business was part of the spirit of reform at the time, as championed by President Theodore Roosevelt and a host of scientists, novelists, and assorted reformers. At that time and in that atmosphere, the hostility of many government regulators toward business was born. Since then, the tone of business-government relations has been generally adversarial. Regulators have tended to be suspicious of the motives of the regulated firms, often because those firms are reluctant to come into voluntary compliance with regulatory policy.

In later years, agencies such as the Federal Trade Commission (during the Carter administration especially) have been perceived as actively antibusiness in their vigorous pursuit of public policy. The animosity between the public and the private sectors has waxed and waned with public moods and economic conditions, but, in the main, conflict rather than cooperation has prevailed in the field of public regulation, resulting in protracted litigation and periodic overregulation. The use of positive incentive systems has been very rare, and efforts at conflict resolution are sporadic and often merely symbolic.

During other political periods vigorous regulation has been compromised by leaders friendly to business. Politicians, anxious to aid their business supporters, have sometimes undermined the efforts of regulatory officials by extending specific favors and exemptions. However, until the election of Ronald Reagan, regulation seemed the primary official governmental approach to business, whatever deals might occasionally be made for the sake of political expediency. The 1980 election put deregulation on the national political agenda for the first time.

Deregulation was one of President Reagan's prime commitments, and he took office in 1981 determined to restore business to a friendly relationship with government. Under the banners of "deregulation," "regulatory relief," "cost-benefit analysis," and "budgetary reform," the Reaganauts "hit the ground running" when they arrived in Washington, committed to assist President Reagan in achieving his goal of "getting the government off our backs." The early selection of such people as Interior Secretary James Watt and Environmental Protection Agency (EPA) Administrator Anne Gorsuch was intended to speed the process of deregulation as they led the way in implementing the administration's policy of cutting back on regulatory activity in almost every field. In the process vigorous regulators were discouraged and discredited whenever possible.

That Reagan consciously intended to change the relationship between government and business is beyond question. He appointed to head most of the regulatory agencies individuals who were pledged to pursue a probusiness line. At first he even planned to abolish the Department of Energy and the Department of Education. Many of Reagan's appointees had, in fact, been open advocates of probusiness and antiregulatory positions. James Watt, who was appointed to head the Department of the Interior, had been the head of the Mountain States Legal Foundation, a group that was primarily active in challenging various aspects of governmental environmental regulations. Anne Gorsuch, Reagan's first head of the Environmental Protection Agency, had worked with a number of Colorado groups opposed to most EPA programs. James R. Harris, Reagan's first chief of the Office of Surface Mining, was so tied to the coal interests that conflict of interest charges were raised during his confirmation hearings. Reagan's choice for the chairmanship of the Equal Employment Opportunity Commission, William M. Bell, although a black person, seems to have opposed affirmative action programs.

Generally, the Reagan strategy of appointing antiregulatory and probusiness administrators was too extreme for members of Congress from both parties. Most of the vanguard of the first round of appointees left government, largely because their relationships with business turned out to be too embarrassingly close or, in some cases, virtually collusive. In their wake were left some demoralized and decimated agencies and, in many cases, quite a permissive view of regulation. By 1986 the major work of "regulatory reform" and "deregulation" was over. The Reagan revolution had restored business to a special relationship with government. Yet, surprisingly, many forms of control of business were still in place, and most of the adversarial features were retained. Congress and the public had not been willing to move quite as far as the administration had wanted to in order to make government a close partner of business. Many of the key features of social regulation lived on, albeit in diminished form.

President George Bush did not continue the Reagan campaign against the regulatory agencies. The Bush administration, confronted by environmental disasters, was less vigorous in its pursuit of deregulation, and the counterappointment strategy was usually avoided. President Bush quickly became aware that the deregulation campaign of his predecessor may have been immoderate. The vast sums of money lost and squandered during the Reagan administration's reduced oversight of the savings and loan industry became an embarrassment to President Bush and to both political parties. The extremely costly savings and loan fiasco thus blunted the drive toward further deregulation. Many political leaders, anxious to distance themselves from the scandals attached to the savings and loan industry, have advocated severe criminal punishment for the misdeeds of bankers during the era of lessened regulatory scrutiny. Other political leaders have called for more stringent regulation of the securities industry, the futures market, and the oil companies. However, healthy corrections of excessive deregulation should not be allowed to slip into another period of overregulation caused by media attention to improper business activities. Instead, the time has come to consider alternatives to regulatory compulsion.

In retrospect, the vast federal programs of loan guarantees to private banks, savings and loans, credit unions, farms, small businesses, and other enterprises were in a very precarious position. According to the Office of Thrift Supervision and the Office of Management and Budget (*Newsweek* 1990), the federal government is currently responsible for $6.6 trillion in other people's debts. Under a system of interactive compliance only a few highly reliable and internally self-regulated companies would be certified and given the privilege of federal loan guarantees. It is not too late to learn this lesson and to begin the process of federal certification. The indictment and prosecution of savings and loan frauds and cheats must continue, but more vigorous prosecution will not cure the problem. Indeed, Attorney General Richard Thornburgh has said that it can take four years to develop a case and bring it to successful conclusion. Even working with an enlarged prosecutorial budget, the Justice Department can pursue only a mere handful of "priority action" cases (Thornburgh 1990, F7). Prosecution after the harm has been done is not an adequate deterrent to business cheats, and it is not a sufficient protection to taxpayers.

Still, President Reagan had a point. Regulation had become burdensome and excessive in the 1960s and 1970s. A better way of dealing with conflict between the public and the private sectors was needed. But even enlightened members of the Reagan administration had limited success at creating a better working environment for business-government relationships. When he took office in 1984, EPA Administrator William D. Ruckleshaus said he wanted to develop alternative ways of resolving environmental disputes. Yet 80 percent of the 300 regulations issued each year by EPA end up in court (*National Journal* 1986). We believe that it is possible for the EPA to promote better self-regulation of business, and we were pleased that in 1990 EPA's

Region Six launched a program of awards to recognize exemplary management compliance programs. We hope that such programs can reduce the adversary nature of environmental regulatory activity, and we look forward to seeing the results of Region Six's pilot program.

For the most part, business advocates continue to pressure Congress to modify the rules of regulatory agencies, and the enforcement branches of those agencies are constantly embattled in their efforts to encourage or compel compliance with regulations. This adversarial mode of business-government relationships in the regulatory arena can be adapted to a more cooperative, less confrontational mode through positive interaction between compliance officials from the public and the private sectors. This mode of cooperation has been termed "interactive corporate compliance" (Sigler and Murphy 1988). The central theme of interactive corporate compliance is the encouragement of effective compliance systems within each business so as to ensure that the purposes of public policy are reflected in the internal operations of American businesses—not only through the threats of enforcement efforts for noncompliance, but also through the positive effects of recognition of the obligations to make corporate practices square with the requirements of public policy. Voluntary compliance can be made palatable, and even profitable, in an effective scheme of interactive compliance.

It seems clear that regulatory compliance can be better achieved by taking an interactionist approach. One recent empirical study showed that state food inspectors could gain greater compliance through persuasion than through threats or formal enforcement actions (Frank and Lombness 1988). The use of incentive systems to encourage compliance with environmental regulation has been extensively explored by Barry Mitnick (1980). In fact, Mitnick has been proposing some form of incentive system for public organizations at least since 1977 (Mitnick, Backoff, and Rainey 1977).

The use of positive reinforcement and persuasion needs even broader application in the regulatory arena than Mitnick has suggested. In fact, with the Sigler and Murphy interactive compliance measures (1988), based on a system of governmental certification of high-complying companies as models of public responsiveness, regulation need not be fought out in an arena, but can be implemented in a setting of greater cooperation between the public and the private sectors. Thus, the public interest will be served without substantial threat to the economic health of our industries.

The main point of contact between business and government is the civil servant who enforces and interprets regulations. At this point, mutual suspicion is at its height, but it is also at this point that more can be done to encourage a cooperative and flexible relationship between business and government. Career civil servants are the workhorses of the regulatory system. Their attitudes, although influenced by the policies of their superiors, tend to pervade the long-term memory of the administrative state. For this reason it is important that career civil servants support and spread the ideals of interactive compliance. They are the key actors in the daily governmental interface with business, and interactive compliance depends on their support.

Interactive compliance is a means of changing the behavior of the overwhelming majority of corporate executives who are not crooks or cheats. Public regulation aims to change the behavior of companies and corporations in directions deemed to advance the public good. Reward and recognition for internal corporate efforts to monitor, redirect, and correct deviant activities will encourage decent managers to take those steps that they know the law requires without losing their competitive edge to less scrupulous competitors. There will always be company executives and other employees who deserve punitive treatment. But rhetoric about corporate social responsibility or business ethics is too bland to change corporate behavior; only stringent enforcement will discourage unscrupulous executives. However, government must learn to discriminate between those corporate actors who accept their public obligations and those who skirt them.

Business ethics are not enough, although some regard ethics codes as an effective means of corporate self-regulation (White 1980). There have been more recent studies of corporate ethics policies (Business Conference Board 1990), but little has changed in the past decade. In 1980 Southern Methodist University released a study of the ethical policy statements of 174 American corporations. Most of these statements were five pages or less in length and were concerned primarily with day-to-day issues affecting the actions of corporate executives and employees. Over half the corporations studied had statements on specific issues, such as bribes, gifts, and payments to or from governmental employees, customers, and suppliers. Compliance with federal and state laws was frequently included in these statements as an additional obligation. Few corporate statements mentioned corporate obligations to American society (Southwestern 1980). The very fact that major corporations have addressed such issues is an encouraging sign, and interactive corporate compliance would build on and reinforce such initiatives. But these statements do not ensure that corporations will police their own moral and legal conduct. They show a refreshing concern for ethics and legality, but more is needed to implement these statements. What is needed is a systematic effort to reinforce socially desired behavior by recognizing and rewarding those companies that are not frozen into conflicting relationships with government and that are willing to develop the kinds of compliance systems that can translate vague talk of business ethics into practical consequences to protect the health, safety, and economic security of the public.

Many business administration scholars have attempted to reduce regulatory conflicts through the inculcation of corporate ethics and values. Professor William C. Frederick of the University of Pittsburgh has collected empirical research on the topic (1987) and has written about the future development of corporate social responsibility (1983). A newer business literature addresses attempts to deal with business ethics as an aspect of corporate strategy (Freeman and Gilbert 1988). Of course, Lee Preston and James Post's pioneering work in this field remains the essential classic statement (1975).

Viewed from a public perspective, the issue is not fostering corporate social responsibility, but adopting the best techniques to secure needed changes in corporate behavior. If the public, through its elected officials, insists on a higher standard of business performance than is deemed desirable or affordable by businesspersons, steps must be taken by government agents to persuade or compel compliance. But compulsion is often a poor motivator. The best means for insuring compliance with public policy is a reliable internal system that identifies, tracks, audits, and corrects infractions of laws and rules. Each business that can produce such a certified self-regulating compliance system deserves greater trust and less suspicion from the public sector. A premium must be placed on self-regulation by responsible corporations, reserving harsh enforcement efforts for the recalcitrant companies that regularly flout the law.

John Braithwaite is one of a few scholars who has made empirical studies of how corporations regulate themselves. He feels, as we do, that "libraries are filled with corporate ethics books," but "what companies do and how they are structured to channel behavior in prescribed directions is ultimately more important than what they say they should do" (1985b, 39). He also believes that to be effective, compliance measures must involve the top levels of management. There must be a "free route to the top" for any employee who is aware of corporate wrongdoing or suspicious conduct. We concur with Braithwaite's finding that companies with high compliance records will incorporate compliance practices into the overall evaluation of managers for promotion or bonus (Braithwaite 1985b, 51).

One of the best studies of a specific industry is Braithwaite's examination of the enforcement of laws concerning coal mine safety (1985a). This issue is one of enormous social consequences. Over 100,000 American miners have been killed in mine accidents in this century. Even more may have died of black lung disease. But the number of miners who have died each year has been sharply reduced: In 1907, 3,241 American miners died from accidents; in 1983, the figure was 70. This reduction was due in part to improvements in mining technology, but it is more attributable to enforcement of laws and regulations, many of which were resisted at first by mine owners.

Braithwaite concludes his study of 39 coal mine disasters around the world with the observation that the enforcement of coal mine safety laws has been a major factor in the decline of fatalities and serious injuries (1985a, 173). Tough enforcement has produced good results, but enforcement, he says, must encompass an appropriate mix of punishment and persuasion to obtain maximum compliance. Punishment alone will not deter noncompliance, but punitive measures must always be available to have effective compliance.

In general, Braithwaite concludes that "when there is willingness to do the right thing, across-the-board punishment is simply not the best strategy for maximizing compliance," although "punishment is the best strategy when good will is wanting" (1985a, 99). Corporations or their executives should be punished only when more positive methods are unavailing. For this reason Braithwaite argues that a purely punitive, adversarial approach to business regulation will not gain widespread compliance. In fact, "the price [agencies] must pay for indiscriminate use of punishment is lower compliance, because by remorselessly punishing those with a genuine desire to comply, we alienate them" (1985a, 100). These observations and conclusions rest on extensive empirical documentation.

We agree with these insights of Braithwaite and have constructed the outlines of a system of persuasion and cooperation that goes well beyond an adversarial approach toward business regulation. While mindful of the continuing need to have the hammer of tough sanctions available to deal with persistent noncompliance, interactive corporate compliance prefers to emphasize the possibilities for a more positive compliance environment than is presently seen in the United States. Without fully endorsing our particular scheme for interactive compliance, Braithwaite supports the basic approach that we are advancing. He believes that self-regulation should be tried before enforced self-regulation and that command regulation should be tried only after the first two approaches have failed. When the government is locked into adversarial, punitive enforcement policies, as agencies responsible for mine safety regulation are, the likelihood that violations will be influenced by regulation is small. On the contrary, a purely punitive environment encourages evasion and concealment since there is limited incentive to behave in acceptable ways.

A subtle, flexible enforcement policy will include both positive and negative approaches. Interactive corporate compliance is a systematic approach to positive reinforcement of compliance. We believe that the Murphy-Sigler interactive corporate compliance approach is more self-enforcing than is any other that has been proposed. It will work because it is based on a pragmatic balancing reward system. The problem is to provide adequate rewards within a comprehensive certification system.

The use of government certification as a part of a voluntary compliance program has been a cornerstone of one program of the Occupational Safety and Health Administration (OSHA). The Voluntary Compliance Program (sometimes called the Voluntary Protection Program) was launched by OSHA in 1982. Since then it has succeeded in reducing accident rates and increasing productivity in the certified firms. Those firms have received the positive incentive of reduced inspections. According to the chief of the program, OSHA has provided industry models of what can be achieved, a "nucleus of cooperation that can lead to consensus standards" without adding to budget or personnel (Richardson 1986, 2). Only a few firms have met OSHA's high certification standards, and it remains to be seen whether this program will thrive in later years. Nonetheless, the Voluntary Compliance Program seems to be working well both for OSHA and for the certified companies. The expansion of the program is described in Chapter 4.

From the management side there is evidence of a growing interest in developing the competence needed to produce a reliable self-monitoring system. One approach, environmental auditing, seems to be out ahead of most techniques (Cutler 1983). Antitrust internal compliance systems are even more well developed (see, for example, Comegys 1986; Garret 1978; Leary 1977; Lipson 1971; and Whiting 1962). The Foreign Corrupt Practices Act [P.L. 95–213 (1977)] mandates a form of corporate self-monitoring in dealings between American businesses and foreign governments. In addition, the requirements of equal employment opportunities laws have spurred the creation of self-monitoring systems in industry.

John T. Scholz has also argued that enforcement strategies that encourage voluntary compliance can improve regulatory efficiency. Scholz writes from a regulatory agency perspective, asking whether there can be an increase in cooperation with regulated firms through greater use of voluntary compliance programs. Scholz notes that overly stringent rules result in an increase in compliance costs to regulated firms, so that at a certain point overly stringent rules and adversarial enforcement policies become counterproductive and firms take chances as evaders. Scholz proposes a "tit-for-tat" strategy, which, in a very rudimentary way, resembles interactive corporate compliance. This strategy is based on a game theory model and suffers from the abstraction that comes from such academic exercises. "Tit-for-tat" means that the agency would "cooperate only as long as the firm cooperated" in a reciprocal reward-and-punishment fashion. The agency would set a minimal level of compliance and use its "less rigorous enforcement routines against any firm that met the minimal compliance level in the previous period" (Scholz 1984b, 393). This very short-term approach may work well in the laboratory or the lecture room, but it seems to us insufficient for motivating compliance without a much more detailed set of expectations. We do not disagree with the conclusions Scholz has reached, but his methods for gaining compliance are not defined with the clarity necessary to provide guidelines for business managers. Also, in our view, a scheme of certification based on a proven and reliable system of internal self-regulation will work much better than will a series of limited acts of cooperation. Scholz also misses our point that such a certification process effectively promotes voluntary compliance by requiring both the regulators and the regulated to agree on reasonable and realistic standards for compliance.

Some reformers go far beyond interactive corporate compliance in their efforts to reshape business-government relationships in the United States. Drastic measures that reorganize the internal structure of American corporations have been proposed. We do not believe that such measures are needed or will be effective to correct corporate behavior.

Our disagreement with Ralph Nader's conclusions is most profound. Nader, despairing of the possibility of making corporations act with a sense of social responsibility, advocates the federal chartering of corporations. Major corporations would then have to apply to a federal chartering agency. Such a charter would increase internal corporate democracy and the personal liability of managers for corporate acts. In addition, it would establish the duties of the corporation with regard to the society, meaning that environmental, safety, antitrust, and other public policies would be drafted into the corporate charter. These distinct national charters would thus tighten the national government's grip on corporate actions.

Actually, Nader is not alone in this notion. Even Theodore Roosevelt once pressed for federal incorporation, as have many other business reformers before his time and after. Many bills to this effect have been submitted to Congress, but they have never gotten anywhere. Probably this remedy is understood to be inappropriate to a capitalist society, although there may be some support for it in the future. At present, we believe that interactive compliance is a less drastic policy, open to experimentation and fine-tuning, while federal incorporation is likely to raise a political firestorm that may be difficult to control. The conversion of private corporations into semipublic entities seems like a last resort for a free society. Moreover, it raises significant practical risks by fundamentally altering an economic organism that has proved to be an efficient producer of goods and services. The specter of boards of directors deadlocked by political disputes or of managers afraid to reach decisions for fear of individual liability is totally unappealing to a nation concerned about its international competitiveness.

Similar criticism pertains to proposals for increased employee ownership and most other forms of wholesale restructuring of corporate boards of directors. Many academics who criticize private business have sought to reform the corporation by major internal surgery. In our view, just a few changes in corporate governance are needed to help ensure that top executives understand the legal environment of the corporation and to encourage their efforts to bring the corporation into compliance.

Changes in corporate governance have been proposed by many, but the most thoughtful ideas have come from Christopher Stone, whose 1975 book *Where the Law Ends* is regarded as a classic in this field. Stone would have a government-appointed public interest director serve on the board of every major American corporation. This public interest director would have an investigative staff to dig out hard information on the activities of the corporation, especially as these activities related to the legal obligations of the corporation. In other respects, the public interest director would be part of the corporate governance team and would be concerned with corporate growth and profits.

This public interest director would be appointed by the government, but would have to be acceptable to the corporation. Loyalty to the corporation would prevent this director from turning over damaging information to the government, unless the company showed itself unwilling to rectify its mistaken or illegal policies. This conflict of interest would seem to be a genuine limitation on the activities of a public interest director. He would be a virtual governmental spy and a member of a private policy-making board at the same time. This proposal seems to stem from the same movement toward consumer power that Ralph Nader headed, and it suffers from the ideology of consumerism, which is not the same as the ideology of private business. The built-in inconsistency of the position of the public interest director has been pointed out by Demaris (1974, 442). We do not believe that corporations can be compelled to change behavior by the imposition of government-appointed directors.

Stone later advocated a less drastic solution for the development of corporate compliance practices. Rather than public interest directors of corporations, Stone urged the use of punitive damages and large fines as a lever to induce compliance. Monetary penalties are preferred over mandatory internal compliance controls as a general strategy. In Stone's view, monetary penalties are more flexible, more visible, and a greater inducement to compliance because they place the burden of action on corporate managers who must devise cost-effective means for deciding on corporate conduct. A very stiff fine or penalty works as a tonic to clarify the thinking of a manager. Compliance, Stone believes, should rest on such monetary penalties, rather than on some type of internal self-control mechanism because corporations understand money as an incentive—and a disincentive. While Stone leaves open the question of the individual liability of corporate agents, he clearly wants to modify corporate behavior by means of the use of stiff monetary penalties. Techniques such as those advocated here in the name of interactive corporate compliance are regarded by Stone as less effective and less discriminating (Stone 1981). But corporation bashing is not an effective compliance strategy. Moreover, there are increasing doubts about the wisdom of using litigation and liability to mold corporate behavior (Huber 1988).

The limits of any compliance system can be grasped by examining the field of environmental regulation, which has produced some of the most extensive efforts to develop compliance programs. The best study of compliance efforts in environmental regulation concludes that violations have continued and may have increased in number, asserting that "there is no single lever that government agencies can pull, no single strategy that American business can promote, which will result in compliance with our pollution controls and environmental protection laws" (DiMento 1986, 188). Joseph DiMento, who examined corporate compliance with environmental law with great conceptual skill, does admit that more can be done by government to communicate government enforcement policy and to assist support groups within the corporations, but he still believes that inspection and monitoring are vital and that "surprise inspections" are needed to keep companies on their toes.

In spite of the many useful insights of Professor DiMento, much more can be done to assist support groups within corporations than he recognizes. The development of a support constituency is one of the central features of the notion of interactive corporate compliance. DiMento holds no such hope. Instead, his best reform proposal is to tailor the use of sanctions to the apparent motivation of the violator. This would require regulators to determine who within the firm was responsible for violations and to assess the general industrywide norms. It is not clear how government agencies would be able to make such determinations (DiMento 1986, 178–79). However, DiMento does agree that much more could be done by government agencies to promulgate the law in such a way that business understands what is expected. For this, he recommends participation in rule making as an "avenue to clarity" (DiMento 1986, 106–108), but admits that participation will not produce consensus on the meaning of regulatory goals.

The literature on compliance is just beginning to emerge. The data collection that is needed has not yet been done for most regulatory fields. There are many studies of criminal behavior, based on the work of academic sociologists and criminologists, but these are inconclusive. The DiMento book, mentioned above, is based on interviews with executives about their firm's reactions to a charge of noncompliance and about their general attitudes toward securing compliance. DiMento also interviewed environmental agency officials. More such empirical studies are needed, but we believe that companies' self-monitoring systems must be examined in greater depth. The degree to which government can rely on effective self-monitoring is not known, but must be understood in order to make interactive corporate compliance effective. Experiments such as those described later in this book will help develop optimal self-monitoring activities.

Corporations are collective entities; each may have a distinctive culture, yet each lacks a single set of desires and motivations. The collective corporate pursuit of profit is socially acceptable, but public policy imposes a public interest on corporate actors and their shareholders, directors, and employees. The ability of the corporation and its members to grasp the meaning of the public interest, as found in the laws and regulations that define that interest, is limited. However, once the corporate actors have grasped the meaning of those laws and regulations, they must make attempts to translate the public interest into methods of operation within the corporate framework. Some corporate officials and employees are crooks and must be treated accordingly. Most are just people trying to get a job done. They need to understand that they have public duties to perform as well as private obligations to their employers. And they must be provided with tools to guide the conduct of the corporation.

An interactive corporate compliance environment is attainable. We believe that corporate leaders could see the wisdom of undertaking positive compliance programs, rather than expending increasing amounts of corporate revenue on avoidance measures. The costs of finding loopholes and hiring legal staff to resist and fight regulations could be reduced in an interactive environment. Fewer dollars should be devoted to lobbying and public relations campaigns against regulations. Compliance officers in corporations would be given more authority and responsibility in this new environment. Education for compliance would receive priority endorsement from the highest levels of the corporation. But a corporate commitment to interactive compliance will depend on balance-sheet considerations. These must be real gains to the corporation and a new attitude on the part of government regulators.

Administrative agencies would have to give more emphasis to cooperation and to rewards for cooperating corporations. Federal agencies would have to spend more of their time and energy to construct training programs for compliance. They would also have to develop an inventory of compliance materials and make these easily available to companies requesting them. Companies that cooperate with regulatory agencies and seek their help in constructing compliance systems should be rewarded by special considerations, including greater leniency, less oversight, and fewer reporting requirements. On the other hand, uncooperative corporations should be subjected to greater scrutiny and stricter measures. In this way government regulators would be promoting desired behavior for the public interest. While enforcement measures would always be available for use against rule violators, interactive corporate compliance emphasizes reinforcement of those who live within and accept the rules. The success of a government agency should not be measured solely in terms of the number of enforcement actions that result in punishment, but, in an interactive environment, by the number of companies that participate with government in the design of an effective corporate compliance system.

More successful compliance efforts must be based on the development of a rational use of positive and negative sanctions. Interactive corporate compliance proposes that attention be given to the positive self-monitoring efforts of corporations to meet public expectations. Negative sanctions must always be available and can never be weakened. The appropriate mix of negative and positive sanctions cannot be known until such systems are tried extensively and the results measured accurately. Interactive compliance calls for empirical testing of regulatory and compliance techniques in controlled situations, not for reliance on intuition or theoretical generalizations. Professor Braithwaite has paved the way with his pioneering studies of corporate compliance systems. The future of public regulation lies in experimentation with interactive corporate compliance, not with deregulation or with more intensive punitive campaigns directed against businesses. The task that lies ahead is the search for and the discovery of effective compliance tools. This task must engage the best minds in business, government, and the academic community.

There has been a battle of the books over the scope of government deregulation. This is still essentially an "adversary economy," with government and business usually at odds (Marcus 1984). But it is unlikely that deregulation or re-regulation will cure all social ills. Business has been able to use its political power to gain a more "friendly," less combative regulatory environment during the years of the Reagan presidency. Conservative and liberal commentators have been fighting trench warfare under the banner of deregulation or, on the opposite side, under that of the public interest in retaining regulations. There is another choice that has no ideological roots. Now interactive corporate compliance should be attempted to cool off the adversity and to resolve conflicts between regulatory agencies and the regulated without compromising the public interest.

In 1988 we proposed certain legislative measures to promote interactive corporate compliance by providing market incentives for high-complying corporations. We proposed that Congress remove the treble damages features of the antitrust laws for those companies that have attained federal certification. We proposed that federal certification be taken into account in reducing liability in damages actions. We advocated other rewards, such as contract preferences and reduced reporting requirements for certified industries. We advocated absolute protection for the internal reviews of federally certified companies so that these internal reviews could not be used against certified companies in litigation. In 1988 we called on the federal regulatory agencies to promulgate more material to inform and train businesspersons in order to meet their legal requirements. Moreover, we proposed that federal regulatory agencies provide reliable advice to businesses in advance of enforcement activities. Looking backward, we adhere to all these recommendations. Indeed, we are pleased to report that no reviewers, no commentators, and no federal officials have directly disputed or challenged this approach, even though it has had fairly wide distribution. However, we recognize that the first steps toward defining the elements of federal certification are just being taken. Once the elements of certification can be established, the legislative agenda can be advanced. Ultimately certification must confer tangible business benefits. While we do not see businesspeople as villains, we also do not expect them to be angels.

2

Three Enforcement Strategies

Robert Abrams

Fostering ethical business practices is not a new concern.[1] Witness the injunctions in the Old Testament against stealing, lying, and bribery. And the Talmud warns that when a person gives an accounting for his life in front of "the heavenly court," the first question will be whether he conducted his business dealings in good faith. The need to set and obey rules for ethical business conduct is a root principle in the Judeo-Christian heritage that guides our Western culture.

In casting one's eye back over the centuries, it would be nice to be able to say that someone has invented some sort of measuring scale, graduated in units of honesty, that would permit us to measure the conduct of tradespeople of several millennia ago and the conduct of our contemporaries in the business world today. Then we could see whether we have made any progress or not.

I cannot pretend to have done that, but I can say that the struggle to ensure high standards of ethical business conduct is being waged today in a vastly more complex business and social environment than that faced by our counterparts in ancient times. In today's world, judgments about right and wrong are not simple.

One of the more insightful commentators on the ethical dilemmas of our times is Michael Josephson, director of the Josephson Institute for the Advancement of Ethics. Josephson finds a high degree of desire to behave ethically among businesspeople and other professionals in this country (1989). And he finds, if opinion polls are to be believed, that each professional group has a high opinion of its own conduct, especially when compared to other groups. Journalists think they are more ethical than politicians. Politicians believe they are more principled than businesspersons. And everybody thinks themselves pure as the driven snow when compared to lawyers!

Josephson wrestles with an intriguing conundrum: How is it that journalists or politicians or lawyers or businesspeople can all sincerely believe themselves to be ethical when, in the eyes of the rest of society, they are not? His answer is that every professional group or class has a basic, fundamental goal that is imbued with the qualities of an ethical principle or code of conduct, so that it becomes, in Josephson's phrase, that profession's "moral imperative."

This moral imperative is quite distinctive to each profession—for journalists it is advancing the people's right to know; for lawyers, it is winning for the client. And in each case, while the goal sounds good and is hard to dispute, adherence to it can serve to justify conduct that the rest of society finds truly appalling—reporters looting people's garbage cans or lying about their identity to gain information, lawyers making frivolous motions merely to delay a just outcome or embarrassing witnesses during cross-examination by dredging up totally irrelevant details about their personal lives.

For the businessperson, Josephson identifies the moral imperative as the survival of the firm or maximizing profits for shareholders. Again, these goals have an apparently unselfish quality to them, but, in fact, they can be used to justify totally self-interested actions taken in naked pursuit of personal profit or professional advancement.

To be sure, business leaders do need to strive for stability and higher profits, but when pursuit of these goals becomes the highest moral mandate, it becomes acceptable to violate the ethical or legal norms the rest of society would impose. So, for example, skimping on product quality, using fraudulent bookkeeping procedures to meet profit targets, and evading environmental or safety rules could all be accommodated as ethical behavior if they are seen as necessary to pursue a higher moral goal.

The topic of ethics in business can be defined as the search for ways of broadening the moral imperative in the business world. Compliance with the laws and ethical standards established by the rest of society must be seen as an integral element in serving the goals of corporate stability and profits. I have several strategies to suggest in that direction. Before I discuss those, let me stress that corporations have made enormous progress toward ethical business conduct since the robber barons and the earlier decades of the Industrial Revolution.

The days when dozens of coal mine cave-ins and explosions killed hundreds of miners a year, or when nasty toxic effluent from factories could be emptied directly into lake and rivers, or when tainted meat from diseased animals was routinely ground into our breakfast sausage are long past in this country. The ethic that permitted such wantonly reckless behavior, so directly and obviously hurtful to health and safety, has been almost completely overthrown

It is not only in comparison with a century ago that we see dramatic progress. In just the last twenty years, major technological improvements had reduced worker exposure to asbestos, increased automobile safety, and limited the quantities of toxic chemicals carelessly dumped into the environment. Also, despite the pressures of our free market economy, U.S. corporations are among the leaders anywhere in the world in terms of meeting their social and ethical responsibilities. Certainly the contrast with Eastern bloc countries is dramatic. As the Iron Curtain is lifting, the rampant corruption and the gross environmental destruction caused by officials supposedly dedicated to serving the social good have helped put the lie to the promise of communism. Our free-market, capitalist system, coupled with democratic political institutions that provide a check on unbridled greed, has enormous superiority—both in economic *and* in ethical terms—and this has never before been etched in such sharp relief.

While the across-the-board advances in business ethics are significant, news headlines continually remind us that we are dealing with a real and continuing problem. The insider trading scandals on Wall Street, the bribery of government officials to get quick approval of generic drugs or favorable action on defense contracts, and the growing savings and loan scandals—these are all examples of the continued willingness of too many in the business world to sacrifice principles for profit.

I cannot offer a complete global solution to the problem of corporate misconduct, but I would like to offer three possible strategies that would enable us to make continued progress toward that goal. Each strategy can be illustrated by examples in the area of environmental protection—which is appropriate since environmental protection is an area in which government enforcers and the business world increasingly interact in very complex ways. And protecting the environment happens to be one of my highest personal priorities as attorney general of New York.

The first strategy is by no means new, and, thus, it may be somewhat out of place. But it is undeniable that the tremendous advances in ethical business conduct I mentioned earlier have come about largely because *government* has set standards, by law and by regulation, and *government* has enforced those standards. Whether the result is taking the poisonous lead out of gasoline, or ending the discharge of taconite tailings and countless other pollutants into the Great Lakes, or stopping the dumping of dioxin- and PCB-laced industrial waste along country roadsides, it has been punishment or the threat of punishment by the government that has produced major gains in environmental quality.

I am a strong believer in tough environmental enforcement, and it definitely brings results. Lawsuits filed by my office have led to fifty-one toxic waste cleanups either completed or now in progress, costing the companies responsible some $208 million. I also believe that, in extreme cases, criminal prosecutions against willful polluters are essential, and I authored New York's environmental crimes statute in 1982. Since then, my office has convicted fifty-one corporations and eighty-three individuals of environmental crimes.

If our goal is to reinforce in the business community the notion that complying with the legal standards set by society must be a part of its ethical construct, vigorous enforcement is the first and most basic approach.

My second strategy recognizes that the environmental arena need not always be a *battleground* between government and industry. More than any other task we face, the challenge of protecting and preserving our environment demands public/private cooperation. Neither government nor the business community alone has the resources or expertise to master the complex environmental problems we face. Global warming, acid rain, the solid waste crisis, and the need to prevent the release of toxic chemicals into our air, our water, and our soil—these serious threats to our health and survival call for a partnership between government and business, based on a foundation of enforcement.

Traditional enforcement strategies must be bolstered by new approaches. For example, the "end of pipe" type of regulation—in which government monitors industrial emissions and imposes civil or criminal penalties for violations of discharge limits—carries very high costs. The greatest cost is that we only catch pollution *after* it happens, when cleanup costs will be the highest and, in some cases, when the environmental or public health damage is irreparable. Government encouragement of industry efforts to *prevent* pollution in the first place would give industry more flexibility and control in determining how best to implement preventive measures to avoid an environmental violation.

A preventive enforcement strategy is ultimately in the best interests of business, government, and the public. For business, it can reduce the often sizable costs associated with civil and criminal litigation;

foster more effective, less burdensome ways of complying with the law; and ensure a fair, competitive marketplace in which all companies are playing by the same set of rules. For government, cooperative approaches offer the potential for higher rates of compliance without the need for massive increases in the resources devoted to enforcement. For the public, the benefits of this approach will come in the form of a cleaner environment and fewer misleading or fraudulent business practices.

One crucial aspect of prevention policy that is gaining wider attention is the environmental audit. Comprehensive audits undertaken voluntarily by corporations to assess compliance, to evaluate the effectiveness of management systems, and to assess the future risks of current practices are becoming an essential part of good business practice. While such audits are not usually strictly required by law and while some corporate executives and their counsel worry about their legal consequences and the uses to which they can be put, comprehensive and regular in-house audits are really the wave of the future. A company that ignores their importance will do so at its own long-term risk.

In our legal and regulatory work, we are increasingly encouraging the use of audits as an integral part of prevention programs. For example, my office drafted a bill, which now has the governor's support, to help prevent toxic chemical accidents. More than 4,354 chemical accidents have occurred in New York since 1983, with 26 deaths, more than 790 injuries, and thousands of people dislocated or evacuated from their homes and jobs. The bill[2] would require facilities with significant quantities of hazardous chemicals to undertake "hazard analyses" in order to identify the risk of accidents and to take reasonable steps to reduce those risks to the lowest level possible. The prevention measures required under the bill are modeled after sound management practices developed and applied by many companies around the world. Under this approach, the company would examine potential accident scenarios and then implement plans to ensure that these never occur. When the plan has been prepared, the facility would notify local emergency planning authorities and the state commissioner of environmental conservation.

These limited environmental audits could improve our chances of preventing toxic chemical accidents without being overly burdensome. The accident prevention plans do not have to be filed with government. Every plant would not automatically be inspected. But local emergency planning authorities and the state commission of environmental conservation could spot-check a plan, and the commissioner could even audit a facility that proves to be particularly accident-prone. Violators could be sued civilly or prosecuted criminally.

While it would shoulder additional responsibilities, industry would also benefit from our bill. By reducing the risk of accidents, businesses could avoid costly cleanups, operate more efficiently, and reduce the likelihood of lawsuits. That means fewer damages payments to individuals who sue, less money paid out in fees to attorneys, and stabilized or lower premiums for liability insurance because the number of accidents would be reduced.

More comprehensive audits than those required in our proposed toxic chemical accident prevention bill should be applied by forward-looking companies as a general practice, even if the law does not currently require it. The costs of not operating preventively can be high indeed. For example, Exxon's corporate image and financial situation would be immeasurably better today if it had undertaken a top-to-bottom assessment of its procedures, equipment, and training involved in the refining and transport of oil. The Valdez spill has cost the firm close to $2 billion in cleanup costs to date, with criminal and civil actions against the company still pending and an aroused public still intensely angry over the incident.

In the New York area there were three major spills involving Exxon facilities in 1990 alone, releasing over 600,000 gallons of oil into the Arthur Kill. My office has been involved in civil and criminal investigations of the company's operations since the first spill on January 1. After two more spills in March 1990, Exxon acceded to my request that it suspend operations at its Bayway refinery and its Bayonne transport facility in order to audit all aspects of its petroleum production, storage, and transportation operations, analyzing its management systems, employee training, and other systems designed to avoid, prevent, or mitigate spills. Already, this audit has identified needed improvements to minimize the chances of more spills from the firm's New Jersey operations.

An excellent recent example of this more *proactive* approach is the behavior of IBM at its plant in Endicott, New York. Under the federal Emergency Planning and Community Right to Know Law of 1986 (42 U.S.C. secs. 11,001–50), companies for the first time were required to report on so-called "fugitive emissions." These are routine chemical releases into the air that come from sources other than factory smokestacks. The new reporting requirement revealed that an immense amount of toxic materials—some *2.4 billion tons* per year nationwide—were escaping into the environment from sources other than smokestacks.

IBM's Endicott plant ranked second in New York in the volume of fugitive emissions. But unlike some other companies, IBM did not wait until it was pressed by the federal or state government to take action to solve this problem. The company read the report itself and decided to take its own comprehensive look at its operations to curb these emissions. Most of the releases involved toxic solvents, so the company tried to reduce the amount of solvents used in its production process and to replace them with less toxic materials wherever possible. The company looked at all of its systems and pipes for possible leaks as well. In a fairly short time, IBM has reduced the level of its toxic fugitive emissions by over 50 percent, and it has set itself a goal of 90 percent reduction for the longer term. By taking the initiative to prevent future environmental problems, IBM is ensuring that it will not face the kinds of severe penalties or public disapproval faced by other companies that waited to act until it was too late.

In another example of a preventive compliance strategy, the 3M Company in Minnesota has undertaken almost 2,000 pollution prevention measures and saved an estimated $300 million since 1975 (*Time*, 1989). One of its many cost-saving programs involved redesigning a production process so that toxic solvents *did not* have to be used. Accident prevention of this sort is not only good public policy—it is also good business.

The final strategy I wish to explore is more an observed phenomenon than a conscious strategy. More and more, individual citizens throughout the country are deciding to reward what they see as "good" businesses with patronage, support, and good will and to tell the dishonest or unethical corporations to shape up or lose their business. This is becoming particularly evident in the areas of the environment and public health.

A recent Gallup poll found that 83 percent of those polled have changed their buying or living habits to help protect the environment and that 30 percent have gone so far as to boycott a company's products because of its record on the environment (*Advertising Age*, 1989). Corporate good will and reputation are increasingly on the line in the environmental area, and companies are making efforts to respond.

Some recent examples are encouraging. Conoco's decision to buy double-hulled tankers despite their extra cost was spurred in large part, I believe, by the enormously negative public reaction to the Exxon Valdez spill. The announcement by tuna packers that they would boycott producers who use large, dolphin-trapping nets was clearly done to curry favor with activists who have sounded an alarm over the needless destruction of dolphins. And Apple Computer and other companies are minimizing the use of ozone-destroying CFCs in their production processes.

However, I am disturbed by the cynical attempts of some companies to portray themselves or their products as environmentally friendly when they are not. When plastic garbage bags are emblazoned with the legend "degradable" and, in fact, they do not degrade at all in the landfills where over 85 percent of our nation's solid waste goes, I think that is an out-and-out fraud. A group of eight state attorneys general, including myself, are determined to hold these companies to a high standard for the claims that they make. I thought it perfectly appropriate that the McDonald's Corporation had to suffer the embarrassment of prominent newspaper stories when it withdrew the claim of recyclability for a container for hash-brown potatoes that was never recycled.

I hope this discussion of a three-part strategy for corporate compliance—continued strong government enforcement, a new emphasis on a government-corporate partnership for preventive action, and the emergence of citizen activism as a prod for ethical corporate conduct—advances in some measure our agenda today.

The importance of ethics in corporate behavior and decision making is directly related to the power of the modern corporation to affect the lives of millions of people. In an era of sophisticated high technology, intense global competition, and pervasive media and mass marketing techniques, the stakes involved in corporate decision making are much higher than at any moment in history. A misleading claim designed to get the edge on the competition can deceive millions of consumers. A failure to comply with laws and regulations regarding the handling and discharge of toxic chemicals can poison a community's water supply or increase the risks of cancer to future generations. Insider dealing and financial manipulations can defraud thousands and cost the taxpayers billions of dollars, as we are painfully learning in the wake of the savings and loan scandal.

Because the consequences of wrongdoing by business are so much greater and potentially more damaging in the era of the multinational corporation and the emerging global marketplace, government and business must work together toward what should be common goals: compliance with the law and adherence to the ethical principles underlying the law.

I have suggested steps that government and business can take in the environmental arena to improve compliance and prevent corporate lawbreaking, but this is not the only area in which we can foster greater government-business cooperation in finding the most effective way to ensure widespread adherence to laws and regulations. We should recognize and acknowledge the common interests between government and the vast majority of business leaders in enhancing the benefits of our social and economic order. Corporations, like other entities and citizens, must see themselves as responsible participants in progress, not as social renegades or corner-cutters. Government must see itself not only as a policeman, but also as a facilitator.

We—meaning government, business, consumers, the American public—are all in this for the long haul. Short-term profits and rewards and short-sighted interests more and more often must give way to long-term responsibility and commitment. We cannot afford to play as though we need to win or lose only one game.

This, I believe, is one of the lessons of the late twentieth century and its enormous upheavals, disasters, promises, and hopes. As proponents of the free marketplace, of liberty, of opportunity, and of individual and social responsibility, we Americans have an obligation to learn this lesson as we move forward into the next century.

NOTES

1. Based upon an address by Attorney General Robert Abrams at the Conference on "Preventing Corporate Lawbreaking: New Approaches to Government/Business Interaction," held at New York University's Stern School of Business on April 21, 1990. The conference explored the subjects of business ethics and legal compliance.
2. The Toxic Accident Prevention Bill, Assembly Bill 7418-A (1988–89) was considered but not passed by the New York State Legislature in 1990.

3

Corporate Codes of Conduct and Corporate Self-Regulation

Harvey L. Pitt and Karl A. Groskaufmanis

Corporate codes of conduct fit into no clearly defined legal niche. Few courts have weighed the legal impact of corporate policy statements intended to discourage employee defalcations. By investing in compliance programs, executives reasonably expect that this effort will afford the corporate entity a measure of protection from civil or criminal liability. To their surprise, prevailing legal norms offer little to bolster these expectations.

This chapter proposes an alternative standard of corporate liability when the defendant corporation has developed a meaningful code of conduct. An *effective* program, to some extent, should shield the corporation from exposure. Support for this alternative standard derives from a handful of decisions in which courts considered compliance programs in determining corporate liability; these courts assess whether the compliance programs were tailored to the entity involved, effectively communicated to employees and enforced. The current state of the law often renders futile the investment made in such programs. Rewarding effective programs would foster careful supervision—a fundamental objective of our system of corporate liability.

This chapter reviews the genesis, composition, and legal effect of corporate codes of conduct. The review is presented in four parts. First, we summarize the forces that prompted the adoption of corporate codes. Second, we consider the product of those forces. This section examines empirical studies of corporate codes—including surveys of publicly held companies conducted in 1984 and 1987 by Fried, Frank, Harris, Shriver & Jacobson (Fried, Frank 1984, 1987). Third, from the limited case law addressing such codes, we analyze the trend toward increased judicial willingness to weigh good faith efforts at self-regulation. Finally, from these cases, we propose a standard that scrutinizes closely the day-to-day operation of corporate codes.

THE FORCES PROMPTING CORPORATE CODES OF CONDUCT

Many corporate codes are the product of a crisis environment. A spate of scandals involving widespread corporate misconduct—price fixing in the 1960s, questionable or illegal foreign payments in the 1970s, and defense procurement fraud and insider trading in the 1980s—has provided the impetus for such codes at different times. In each instance of broad-scale corporate misfeasance or malfeasance, the courts and Congress invariably have responded with heightened criminal sanctions to enforce newly articulated, or rearticulated, economic rules. In an effort to avoid such sanctions, or to avoid a repetition of their problems, corporations have responded by adopting codes of conduct.

These codes were not adopted in a vacuum; often corporations heeded persuasive exhortations—or statutory requirements. A presidential commission examining defense procurement directed contractors to "promulgate and enforce codes of conduct that address their unique problems" (President's Blue Ribbon Commission, 1986, 81). The Packard Commission applauded what was termed the "Defense Industry Initiative"—a pledge by signatory contractors to enforce codes of conduct. The Treadway Commission, reviewing fraudulent financial reporting, urged all public companies to adopt codes (*Report of the National Commission for Fraudulent Financial Reporting* 1987, 35).

In some instances, Congress has gone further and mandated codes for securities professionals. Under the Insider Trading and Securities Fraud Enforcement Act (ITSFEA) of 1988, broker-dealers and investment advisors must "establish, maintain, and enforce" written policies and procedures to deter insider trading offenses by "controlled persons" [15 U.S.C.A. sec. 78o(f) (Supp. 1989)]. Previously, the Securities and Exchange Commission (SEC) had adopted

Investment Company Act Rule 17j-1, requiring registered investment companies to "adopt a written code of ethics" to deter fraudulent or manipulative conduct. Consequently, not all corporate codes represent an entirely voluntary exercise of supervisory judgment.

THE COMPOSITION OF CORPORATE CODES

Most empirical research examining such codes is recent; the preface to a 1980 study indicated that it was "believed to be the only such compilation of major corporate policy statements." Fried, Frank undertook two surveys—in 1984 and 1987—to add to this research.[1] From the results of these surveys, we make several observations about corporate codes of conduct.

Today, most public corporations have a code of conduct. Both Fried, Frank surveys found that over 90 percent of the companies polled had adopted some type of code. Other studies indicate that at least three-quarters of the corporations surveyed had adopted such codes (Center for Business Ethics 1986). These results suggest that codes have emerged as standard corporate fare.

While corporate codes are not limited to legal concerns, such issues clearly are a major consideration in their adoption. Three items appear routinely in at least half the codes surveyed. Most common are provisions addressing issues raised by the Foreign Corrupt Practices Act—the impetus for the development of many codes. The most recent Fried, Frank (1987) survey found that 68 percent of the codes addressed antitrust concerns, although a greater disparity in results exists on this issue. Vigorous insider trading prosecution probably influenced the three-quarters of the 1987 Fried, Frank respondents who included this issue in their codes—an increase of 13 percent from their 1984 study.

Empirical research suggests that the greatest shortcoming of corporate codes lies in the inadequacy of compliance efforts. In both Fried, Frank surveys, only one-third of the respondents included formal enforcement procedures in their codes.[2] Although several surveys indicated that a high percentage of the codes addressed enforcement, these numbers can be deceptive. While the authors of one study found sanctions mentioned in 42 percent of the 119 codes surveyed, only 7 of the codes were specific on this issue (Cressy and Moore 1983, 69). A 1980 study went to the heart of the issue by questioning companies with respect to how often penalties were imposed for code violations. Three-quarters of the companies surveyed indicated that they had imposed no such penalties in 1979.[3] The empirical research thus raises doubts about the enforcement of code provisions.

The 1980 study is one of the few to probe companies on the perceived legal effect of such codes. Over three-quarters of the officers surveyed believed that the code afforded protection for the company; 65 percent expected that the code would protect them legally (Opinion Research Corporation 1980, 98). In 1984 Chemical Bank's chief counsel noted that the bank's code of ethics "is more legalistic than we'd like," but the document is "tight enough so we could stand on it in the event of a legal breach" (Ethics Resource Center 1984,4). Corporations appear to adopt codes with the unstated premise that the document may later be invoked for legal protection.

AN EMERGING DUE DILIGENCE DEFENSE

Courts have done little to confirm that corporate codes effectively shield a corporation from liability. "Black letter" legal principles give little weight to an employer's compliance program. Two strands of case law, however, support an alternative standard. First, several courts have given (or endorsed) jury instructions indicating that codes may be considered when assessing corporate criminal liability. A second, more complete articulation of the legal effect exists with respect to Chinese walls—one form of corporate code. The growing acceptance of Chinese walls provides lessons, by analogy, for the implementation of corporate codes.

The prevailing norm in assessing a corporation's criminal liability underscores that a code is not an automatic panacea. A company may be held criminally responsible for its employees' acts "if they were acting within the scope of their authority, or apparent authority, and for the benefit of the corporation, even if . . . such acts were against corporate policy or express instructions" (*United States v. Basic Construction Co.*, 711 F.2d 570,573 [5th Cir. 1983]). Some prosecutors have taken the position that the existence of a corporate compliance program is, as a matter of law, irrelevant. Judicial opinions are divided, but there is authority rejecting this absolute position and holding that corporate policy "may be considered in determining whether the employee in fact acted to benefit the corporation" (*United States v. Beusch*, 596 F.2d 871, 878 [9th Cir. 1979]). These courts require a showing of effective implementation of the code before they will consider affording it any legal significance. "Merely stating or publishing such instructions and policies without diligently enforcing them is not enough to place the acts of an employee who violates them outside the scope of his employment" (*United States v. Beusch*, 596 F.2d 871 at 878).

In some criminal antitrust actions, for example, juries have been instructed to consider whether the defendant corporation "acted diligently in the promulgation, dissemination and enforcement" of antitrust compliances programs. The judiciary's willingness to consider this issue at all marks its recognition of the relevance of corporate codes of conduct to corporate criminal culpability (Miller and Levine 1984, 46).

CHINESE WALLS

Chinese walls are one form of a code of conduct that has received judicial scrutiny in a number of contexts. Chinese walls are institutional procedures that block an organization's internal flow of information. These procedures allow the organization to carry on activities that would otherwise be precluded by a conflict of interest. Over the last twenty years, the Chinese wall has gained increasing support in cases involving securities firms, banks, and law firms.

In the securities context, the Chinese wall has inched closer to the status of an affirmative defense. In the 1968 proceeding in which the Chinese wall made its debut, the SEC was tentative in its endorsement (In Re Merrill Lynch, Exchange Act Release No. 8459 [1968]). Over the next two decades, however, the commission increasingly recognized the utility of Chinese walls. Rule 14e-3, adopted in 1980, created a safe harbor from the "disclose or abstain" rule for firms that had developed procedures to screen individuals making investment decisions. The settlement of insider trading cases often required that institutions improve their Chinese walls. More recently, Chinese walls were in the spotlight when Shearson Lehman acted both as advisor and as equity participant in a hostile transaction. In the ensuing litigation, SEC General Counsel Daniel Goelzer advised the trial judge that "violations of the federal securities laws stemming from [Shearson's potential conflicts of interest] can be avoided through the use of well-established preventive policies and procedures, such as Chinese Walls, restricted lists and watch lists" (*Kopper's Co. v. American Express Co.*, 689 F. Supp. 1371, 1415 [W.D. Pa. 1988]).

Similarly, in *Cotton v. Merrill Lynch, Fenner & Smith, Inc.*, (699 F. Supp. 251 (N.D. Okla. 1988)] the plaintiffs asked the court to disregard the Chinese wall. In that case the plaintiff brokerage customers alleged that the defendant broker-dealer was under a fiduciary duty to disclose material, nonpublic information acquired in its capacity as a financial advisor. The court endorsed a magistrate's conclusion that "courts have established that brokers have a primary obligation not to reveal inside information to clients for the clients' benefit in trading securities (*Cotton v. Merrill Lynch*, 699 F. Supp. at 256). Chinese walls exist to avoid such disclosure. Without mentioning the procedure by name, *Cotton* moved the Chinese wall closer to the status of a legal defense.

Bank Chinese walls—mandated to prevent the misuse of material, nonpublic information by the bank's trust department—have proved helpful in a unique species of litigation. In the late 1970s several banks were sued after agreeing to finance the hostile takeover of a customer. While the outcome consistently turned on the customers' failure "to draw a fiduciary rabbit from a commercial loan agreement hat" (*Washington Steel Corp. v. TW Corp.*, 602 F.2d 594, 600 [3rd Cir. 1979]), the presence of Chinese walls aided the defendant banks in several cases. In another case a federal district court ruled for the bank, finding insufficient proof "that there was, in fact, a breach of the so-called Chinese Wall" (*Harnischfager Corp. v. Paccar*, 474 F. Supp. 1151, 1153 [E.D. Wis. 1979]). These legal victories no doubt led banks to form Chinese walls within departments in order to allow a single institution to offer financing to competing bidders in more recent takeover contests.

The most complete judicial articulation of how a Chinese wall should operate occurs in the context of law firm screening procedures. These procedures are implemented to screen lawyers whose previous employment precludes their participation in a particular case. *Kesselhaut v. United States* [555 F.2d 791 (Ct. Cl. 1977)], the first decision to recognize the Chinese wall defense to law firm disqualification, foreshadowed the procedures that courts would expect. In *Kesselhaut*, the firm had promulgated screening rules, locked the files of the case in question, and limited access to the keys on a "need to know" basis.

Subsequent cases have imposed equally demanding requirements. Thus, the Chinese wall defense has been unavailable when effective procedures are not in place. For example, the U.S. Court of Appeals for the Federal Circuit recently upheld a lower court ruling that observed that "there is a complete lack of evidence before the court indicating that the entire . . . firm was also notified of this oral screening" (*Atasi Corp. v. Seagate Technology*, 847 F.2d 826, 831 [Fed. Cir. 1988]). Moreover, even sufficient procedures will not meet the standard if they are implemented only after an opponent moves to disqualify the firm (*LaSalle National Bank v. County of Lake*, 703 F.2d

252 [7th Cir. 1983]). The requirements of this review would probably carry over to judicial scrutiny of corporate codes of conduct.

LEGAL STANDARDS AND THE DECISION TO ADOPT A CORPORATE CODE

Corporations should view codes of conduct and compliance programs as desirable goals, irrespective of the legal implications of those codes. A litany of good reasons supports the adoption of a corporate code. Internally, the code offers an unambiguous statement of normative standards for those employees who want to conform their behavior to corporate rules. Employees are less apt to violate such rules if they know the company is serious about enforcing its standards. Corporate codes also provide a meaningful message to the public; a corporate defendant is less likely to be viewed with the disdain reserved for lawbreakers when the company in question did all it could to prevent the violation. Moreover, prosecutors at least will consider—even if they will not credit—the existence of an effective compliance program before asserting liability against a company whose carefully formulated and enforced code of conduct has been violated by an errant employee. Consequently, even if the law governing codes remains in its present ambiguous state, the development of corporate codes is likely to continue unabated.

The adoption of a code, however, is rarely a purely voluntary act and is less likely to be a voluntary act in the future. While the decision to develop a code may technically be "voluntary," the ambient circumstances surrounding the adoption of most codes create many subtle—and not so subtle—incentives to foster compliance programs. Moreover, some companies are under a statutory obligation to develop such programs. For example, ITSFEA represents one instance in which Congress required corporations to develop internal standards [15 U.S.C.A. sec. 78o(f) (Supp. 1989)]. Similarly, agencies with prosecutorial power are turning toward codes of conduct as part of the settlement process. These codes, and other examples of corporate self-governance such as internal corporate investigations, are becoming a regular staple among the conditions on which favorable settlements can be based in negotiations with government agencies. Corporate codes of conduct are a product of the pressures created by the current regulatory environment.

The current state of the law deprives society of the benefits that would accrue from widespread state-of-the-art compliance programs. Despite cynicism that is sometimes well grounded, corporate self-regulation provides a valuable check against antisocial behavior. The corporation is in the best position to predict sources of potential misconduct and to develop the most appropriate controls. The controls that the corporation develops are likely to be more efficient than a system imposed by the government. While no system of self-regulation can, or should, exist completely unchecked, corporate self-regulation gives society an additional measure of protection that is worth promoting and facilitating.

Finally, corporate self-regulation provides a superior alternative to tort or criminal liability as a means to effect society's expectations of business. Criminal penalties and burgeoning punitive damages awards exist primarily to shape employer behavior. Corporate liability has widespread social effects. Unbridled tort liability imposes a hidden tax on the American economy; the criminalization of administrative offenses usurps limited prosecutorial resources and adds a harrowing dimension to often murky areas of the law. Corporate self-regulation provides a controlled, efficient, and rational alternative. Common law rules governing the effect of employers' instructions evolved in another era—before the age of corporate codes, compliance departments, employee hotlines, and other procedures adopted by modern corporations. The legal standard should be adapted to this new reality.

REWARDING DUE DILIGENCE: A NEW LEGAL STANDARD

Our proposed standard refines the due diligence defense included in the Model Penal Code (American Law Institute 1985). This defense shields the company if a "high managerial agent" has exercised due diligence in his or her supervisory efforts. The Model Penal Code's approach, one criticism states, fails to take a functional view of the corporation. By focusing on the company's policy-making managers—the "lynchpins"—the defense fails to recognize that corporate misconduct is the product of wayward employees who are insufficiently supervised. Inevitably, the crux of the problem lies further down the line. Critics conclude that the traditional due diligence defense fails to consider the realities of the commission and prosecution of white collar crimes.

This flaw can be corrected by shifting the standard of review to the company's shop floor. This shift, we believe, creates a more reliable test for compliance programs. Instead of focusing on a company's "inner circle," the review should consider the employees at whom the compliance efforts were directed. If a diligent effort was made to develop a policy, this effort should be rewarded by our legal system. We propose a standard that balances the needs to deter misconduct and to promote effective self-regulation.

In order to claim the protection of a modified due diligence defense, a company should first be required to meet a rigorous standard. This review would ensure that the procedures have been implemented diligently and in good faith. By definition, this will be a fact-specific review. Relevant elements to this review include the following:

1. *Burden of Proof.* Because reliance on a code of conduct might entitle a company to an exception from presently existing liability concepts, the corporate defendant should bear the burden of proving the existence of an effective compliance program. This burden should be assessed in light of the fact that, notwithstanding the existence of the compliance program, conduct prohibited by the company's code of conduct occurred. Courts must balance (1) the recognition that even the best and most vigorously enforced compliance program cannot prevent venal employees from violating the terms of such policies with (2) the fact that the existence of violations of corporate policies (particularly if there are repeated instances of such violations) may reflect inadequacies in formulating the policy, selecting and training employees, or supervising the corporate policies in question.

2. *Duration of the Code.* It is relevant in this context to ascertain when the policy in question was adopted. A code of conduct of longstanding duration, adopted in the absence of any particular misconduct, should be given great deference by the courts. Conversely, a code of conduct recently adopted in response to an outbreak of activities that have imposed vicarious liability on the company should be entitled to less deference.

3. *Adoption of the Code.* Courts should take into consideration the process by which the particular corporate code was adopted. A code adopted by management, without the involvement of the company's board of directors, may be entitled to less deference than a code of conduct that has recently received the imprimatur of the company's board and that truly reflects corporate policy.

4. *Scope of the Code.* Companies cannot foresee every possible employee defalcation that might give rise to a claim of vicarious liability. But most companies that have been in business for any substantial length of time can accurately predict the types of activities that are most likely to raise vicarious liability issues over time. As a result, courts should give greater deference to a code that effectively governs the conduct for which liability is in issue. By definition this means the more general the language of the particular code or compliance program is, the less deference the statement is apt to receive, as in *Yates v. Avco Corp.* [819 F.2d 630, 635 (6th Cir. 1987)], in which the court noted that "though the intent of the policy was

commendable, the facts of the case demonstrate that not only was it vague on paper, it was vague and ad hoc in its implementation and did not function effectively. . . ." Nevertheless, courts should understand that undue specificity may create adverse implications.

5. *Clarity of the Code.* A corporation that drafts a compliance program or code of conduct should bear the responsibility for genuine ambiguities in the language and in the interpretation of the document. As noted earlier, a successful code should make it clear what types of conduct are being prohibited and the reasons for imposing the prohibition. Moreover, since the intent of these programs and codes is to avoid inadvertent violations of the code or compliance program, by definition this requires precise articulation and lack of ambiguity in formulating the code of conduct.

Clarity is also essential in connection with the company's statement of disapproval. It should be unambiguous that the company disapproves of the conduct interdicted in the code and that such conduct will be treated as outside the scope of an employee's employment. Employees should have no doubt, based on a reading of the compliance program, that a violation of its terms will subject them to discipline and possible discharge.

6. *Communication to Employees.* Courts should give deference to a code of conduct that is adequately communicated to employees. Adequate communication entails more than a glossy handout to employees (*United States v. Beusch*, 596 F.2d at 878). It requires documents that are treated with respect, that are circulated to employees on their first day of employment, and that are periodically recirculated to employees. It should also require a showing that, in addition to handing employees a compliance manual or code of conduct, the company took the time to explain the code to its employees and had in place a mechanism to respond to employee questions about the substantive or procedural aspects of the code. As an integral part of the process, communication should be a two-way street, and employees should be required to certify periodically that they have read, understood, and complied with the existing code of conduct or compliance program. There should be an immediate follow-up where certifications are not promptly signed and returned.

7. *Periodic Review of the Code.* Another factor that courts should weigh is the attention given to the code of conduct or compliance program after its adoption. Is the code subject to periodic review and amendment, to take account of such factors as (1) changes in the law; (2) the approaches of other, similarly situated companies; and (3) the company's own experience in the administration of the code or compliance program? To the extent that a code of longstanding duration has been adopted, but has never been reconsidered, violations of the

code's policy may reflect the inattentiveness of corporate management, rather than a frolic and a detour on the part of an errant corporate employee.

8. *Effective Oversight of the Code.* Is the corporate code the assigned responsibility of senior management and board personnel? If so, the code should be given great weight by a court as a proper statement of what constitutes the scope of an employee's employment. It is not necessarily sufficient to state that a code has been assigned to the company's general counsel and that its administration is limited to that individual. Board involvement in the process of developing, revising, and overseeing the corporate code or compliance system is a necessity. And there should be something more than perfunctory oversight by board members of each compliance program or corporate code adopted by the company.

9. *Incorporating the Code into the Company's Culture.* Has the compliance program or code of conduct been inculcated into a company's corporate culture? Courts should give great deference to a corporate code that has become a staple of the employees' frame of reference. This means that the distribution of the code, certification of the code, availability of persons to interpret the code, and provision of seminars on the code should be supplemented by routine reminders of the code's existence.

10. *Enforcement of the Code.* Perhaps the most important aspect of this standard is the extent to which the company has been willing to enforce its compliance program or code of conduct. To what extent does the company have in place a mechanism to detect violations of corporate standards before they are discovered or reported by others? To what extent does the company keep track of possible violations of the code? To what extent does the company pursue acknowledged violations of the code? A vigorous self-enforcement program should be the sine qua non of any judicial deference to a corporate code of conduct or compliance program. The modified due diligence standard we propose should take an operational view, requiring the defendant to show evidence of compliance efforts involving the defendant's employees at the particular unit involved in the breach of policy.

The legal standard should create an incentive to develop compliance programs that meet these standards. If the defendant corporation is able to meet these standards, we suggest that an effective program should have a substantive effect in three forums. First, in private tort actions, the program should color a court's assessment of what constitutes an employee's scope of employment. The existence of the procedures should influence—although not necessarily decide—every determination of whether the employee's conduct was within the scope of his or her employment. This does not represent a radical shift from existing law. The greatest impact of this standard in the tort context should be in the "fringes" of civil liability. Meeting these standards should, in virtually all but the most extraordinary cases, shield the company from punitive damages.

Second, an effective compliance program should serve as a defense to administrative proceedings before government agencies. For example, an effective compliance program should rebut a claim that a public company "recklessly disregarded" an officer's insider trading before a major announcement. If the officer received the company's code of conduct, was instructed about the company's trading policy, attended training sessions, and signed a certification of compliance, it would be incongruous to maintain that the company was "reckless."

Finally, the compliance program should operate as a defense against criminal liability. The compliance program would help define when an employee is acting within the scope of his or her employment to benefit the employer. The program makes it clear that the employee could not have intended to benefit the company through his or her acts.

While termed a "modified" due diligence test, the proposed standard would not represent a radical departure from established precedent. In reality, it would merely extend the standard used to review one set of internal procedures—law firms' Chinese walls—to a standard that would apply to all public companies. This standard would rationalize the law of corporate liability and reward prudent behavior.

Beyond that, we suggest that the standard will lead the law of corporate liability to more logical results. Criminal liability will be based on some showing of corporate recalcitrance, rather than on the whims of one employee's actions. While no corporate entity can, without its employees, form a criminal intent, the modified standard will limit prosecutions to corporations that have fostered an atmosphere conducive to criminal activity.

On a different level, a sense of fairness rests at the core of any effective legal system. For the government to recommend—or require—compliance programs and then dismiss them as irrelevant violates that sense of fairness. This is particularly true when a corporation that has developed an extensive program is held liable for the act of an isolated employee. Moreover, failure to provide any credit for compliance efforts could prove frustrating to a manager who may well conclude that it is far simpler to let things take their own course. By contrast, the standard we propose would allow courts to craft equitable results. The benefit a corporation would derive from its corporate code would be proportionate to the effort invested in its compliance program.

CONCLUSION

Our legal system metes out civil and criminal punishment to corporations "to encourage diligent supervision of corporate personnel by managerial employees" (American Law Institute 1985, sec. 2.07, comment 6). Corporate codes of conduct are an important means of establishing supervision. Courts have displayed, and should continue to display, an increased willingness to weigh effective compliance efforts when assessing corporate criminal liability. Few decisions, however, directly address the impact of corporate codes. Although the use of such codes is widespread, their legal effect thus remains an unanswered question. We have proposed a standard that would create an incentive for the development of effective compliance programs. Resolving the current uncertainty shrouding the effect of corporate codes would substantially foster effective self-regulation.

NOTES

1. In 1984 and 1987, the law firm of Fried, Frank, Harris, Shriver & Jacobson surveyed publicly held companies with regard to their codes of conduct. In the 1984 survey 500 companies received questionnaires, and in the 1987 survey 414 companies. The full results of the two surveys may be obtained from the firm on request. It can be concluded from these surveys that codes are rarely invoked in legal proceedings, that most firms have no enforcement procedures to implement their codes, and that just over half of the surveyed firms distribute their codes to all employees.

2. See also Center for Business Ethics (1986). This research concludes that institutional enforcement of ethics codes is very weak.

3. Opinion Research Corporation (1980, 73). But The Conference Board in *Corporate Ethics* (New York: The Conference Board, 1987), 16, reports a survey showing that 61 percent of the companies whose codes provided for termination had imposed that sanction in the previous five years.

4

Leading Examples of Interactive Compliance in Action

Jay A. Sigler

Jay A. Sigler and Joseph E. Murphy, in their earlier book, *Interactive Corporate Compliance: An Alternative to Regulatory Compulsion* (1988), attempted to synthesize business ethics and the field of corporate compliance with laws and regulations. They proposed an approach in which business and government would learn to cooperate with each other to advance social ends through rigorous business compliance programs, developed by businesses in response to a cooperative reward system. Government would reward high-complying corporations with a series of tangible benefits, ranging from less frequent reporting or inspection schedules to tax incentives, contract preferences, and other forms of legal relief. Companies would also benefit economically from the mere fact of government certification and public recognition of their compliance systems. Noncertified companies would be placed at a competitive disadvantage, being subject to greater government scrutiny and more public disapproval. Government, they contended, must learn to discriminate between those corporate actors who accept their public obligations and those who skirt them. In the end, Sigler and Murphy claimed that bridges of trust between the public and the private sectors must be built so that adversary relationships could be diminished and cooperative relationships developed, while also meeting the requirements of public policy. Corporate actors must be convinced that ethical and legal behavior is consistent with good business practice. Regulatory agencies must establish the terms of the trust relationship.

There are very few examples of government programs built on the model of interactive compliance. The best current case is the Voluntary Protection Program (VPP) of the Occupational Safety and Health Administration (OSHA). This program, launched in 1982, has succeeded in reducing accident rates and increasing productivity in certified programs. It is based on a system of government certification of particular plant sites after an exhaustive review of the company's compliance programs, training programs, employee participation, and top management commitment. Those firms that attain the highest level of certification in the so-called "Star Program" receive formal recognition and designation. They may fly flags, display emblems, and otherwise make public display of their government certification. Moreover, they are assured of a special closer working relationship with OSHA, rapid and expedited decision making from the agency, and relief from certain routine government enforcement efforts.

Certification is a valuable prize which is awarded to those industries that exceed the minimal standards set by the regulatory agency. Certified programs go beyond mere literal compliance; they are exemplary cases in which the implementation of high industry standards is rewarded with official recognition. This program seems to be a fine example of building trust between business and government, going beyond formal policy statements about corporate ethics or social responsibility.

To check on the claims made by OSHA, I interviewed Bob Brant, president of the Voluntary Protection Program Participant Association (November 19, 1989). Brant is manager for safety, health, and environmental affairs for Mobil Chemical Company, based in Stamford, Connecticut. He insisted that his corporation had experienced many cost savings as a result of its participation, but that these could not be strictly shown on a balance sheet. He felt that the greater payoffs came in higher employee morale, increased productivity, and a sense of pride in the corporation. According to Brant, these intangibles had dramatically changed the atmosphere and working relationships in the corporation. As a result, his senior management was convinced OSHA's VPP was a top priority, and they conveyed this understanding to corporate employees by direct personal acts, celebrations, plant ceremonies, union recognition, and extensive public relations campaigns. Moreover, Brant himself was assigned the task of working with other industries to get them on board the VPP.

According to Brant, Mobil Chemical could show a continual decline in on-the-job accidents since joining the VPP in 1983. Mobil's accident rate was far below the industry rate in 1983 and continued to decline from that rate. The cost to the corporation of industrial accidents had similarly declined. Moreover, Mobil Chemical has had no OSHA citations since certification in 1983. Fewer employee injuries and illnesses at Mobil Chemical seem to be largely attributable to participation in OSHA's Star Program. Employee involvement in reporting and minimizing potential hazards has been a morale booster as well as a key factor in the Star Program's success. Mobil Chemical's top management is committed to the program and permits substantial employee input in designing safety systems.

However, the OSHA VPP Participant Association that Brant heads is not institutionalized. It has no staff, no newsletter, and no organized bylaws. The organization meets as a whole only once a year at an annual convention. Yet there are plans to make the association a formal professional organization that will conduct lobbying activities and provide rosters of public speakers.

Sixty sites, representing thirty-one different companies, have earned Star Program certification. Mobil Chemical Company has twenty-four certified sites, making it by far the most committed American corporation. Many corporations have just one or two certified sites. Mobil Chemical's strong advocacy of the Star Program is less convincing to some of the other members of the VPP Participant Association, and most American corporations show little willingness to even consider making application for OSHA certification.

When asked why corporations might be reluctant to join the Star Program, Brant suggested that most corporations simply don't trust OSHA. Additionally, bigger companies, familiar with top-down management styles, are uncomfortable with the loss of central management power and initiative that would come with a system requiring active employee participation. Some large corporations are incompletely integrated, so that a few plant sites might have enlightened management, while other units of the same corporation would be reluctant to undertake such experimentation. Perhaps the major impediment is worry about ceding too much power to unions and workers. But, said Brant, the experience of Mobil Chemical was entirely positive, leading to more employee involvement and greater management responsiveness to the ideas of employees. Fully committed corporations gained special working relationships with OSHA that were valuable to the corporation.

Corporate membership in the OSHA Star Program has grown steadily. Very few corporations have dropped out since the program really got going in 1983, and those few dropouts seem to have had other business problems unrelated to OSHA Star Program participation. In 1983 there were just nine Star sites, eight more in 1984, ten more in 1985, twelve more in 1986, eleven more in 1987, and ten more in 1988. The growth seems to be continuing now at about the same rate.

Yet these numbers represent an extremely small percentage of eligible American corporations. Many of the certified sites are within OSHA's Region Six (Texas, Oklahoma, Louisiana, and Arkansas), showing the dedication of that regional administrator to the Star Program. One of the factors that may account for low industry participation is the administrative cost to OSHA in certifying applicants for the Star Program. The twenty-page application is daunting for prospective new members of the Star Program, but it also requires extensive work by OSHA employees to check out each application. A less cumbersome application process could prove an inducement for more companies to make application, while also reducing OSHA's administrative costs. At this moment the Star Program seems to be a limited and fairly elite program within OSHA's operations.

There is no common denominator among the thirty-one Star Program companies. There are companies with as few as fifty employees, and there are giant corporations. It should be noted that there are more chemical companies represented than those of any other industry, which is hardly surprising due to the high risk exposure of such companies. In addition to Mobil Chemical, Dow, Du Pont, General Electric (Plastics Division), Hoechst Celanese, Cain Chemical, SCM Pigments, U.S. Paint, Stauffer Chemical, and Texas Chemical have some certified sites. Georgia Power Company is the only public utility company that is Star certified, Kerr-McGee is the only refining company that enjoys that distinction, and Russell Corporation is the only textile operation to be approved for the VPP. The unusual representation of industry groups may be a clue to the motivations of top corporate managers and to their inclinations to consider participation in OSHA's voluntary program.

OSHA's Voluntary Protection Program is here to stay. In spite of changes in the federal agency and turnover in corporate management, the program is alive and well. Now is the time to spread the word and spread the example. At least, that is what Bob Brant and Mobil Chemical believe. They have expanded the practice of self-enforced compliance programs into other highly regulated areas and are seeking to convince the Environmental Protection Agency (EPA) and other federal regulators to borrow from OSHA's VPP and engage in some form of trust relationship with certified industries. The germ of interactive compliance can be found in this example; pragmatism and good business sense may lead to further experimentation. Yet, it is hard to deny that government regulators and business executives are skeptical of the possibility of devising voluntary self-regulation programs that can be recognized and rewarded by government.

In the field of environmental regulation EPA's Region Six has taken the lead in developing incentives for high compliance. There may have been some communication between OSHA's regional administrator and EPA's regional head, but this can only be inferred from the fact that the two regions overlap in geographic coverage. EPA's Region Six includes Arkansas, Louisiana, New Mexico, Oklahoma, and Texas, while OSHA's Region Six does not include New Mexico. Whatever the impetus may have been, EPA regional administrator Robert E. Layton, Jr., launched his own program in 1988 to recognize "environmental excellence" in regional industries, communities, and businesses.

In a June 23, 1989, EPA press release, Regional Administrator Layton observed, "we cite polluters for violating environmental laws—so I am particularly pleased to recognize industries, communities and businesses for their environmental stewardship." The first such awards went to the cities of Benton, Louisiana and Morgan City, Louisiana for their excellence in wastewater treatment plant operations. The Parish Water Company of Baton Rouge and the community of Jeanerette received EPA's public water supply award. The Valentine Paper Company of Lockport, Louisiana, was the first private industry to receive an award for excellence in industrial wastewater treatment.

The Valentine Paper Company was recognized in 1989 for achieving compliance with its National Pollution Discharge Elimination System (NPDES) required permit for the two previous years. The basis of its selection was a perfect history of effluent compliance, good ratings by the EPA and state inspectors, and compliance with state water rules and federal regulations and policy, as well as an absence of pending or current referrals against the company. Compliance awards are also given for Resource Conservation and Recovery Act (RCRA) hazardous waste compliance on much the same basis. After an EPA/state review and screening for eligibility, the final selections are made by a state committee including state officials, environmental groups, industry and trade associations, and media representatives. The Safety Kleen Corporation won the hazardous waste management award in 1989.

Awards take the form of plaques, flags, certificates, patches, and pins, presented at public ceremonies that are heavily publicized by the EPA. The benefits of the awards program seem obvious. The positive incentive for exemplary compliance complements EPA's enforcement effort. The program encourages outstanding environmental management, but it also promotes professionalism in the environmental work force by recognizing high-quality performance. The fact that the criteria for eligibility must be developed by each program compels the EPA staff to identify the characteristics of high performance. Extensive documentation to support a nomination must also be produced by environmental officials. The public recognition provides a positive forum to communicate environmental goals, while promoting pollution prevention. In time, industries will compete more and more for EPA recognition. Inclusion of industry leaders and environmental groups in the final selection process promotes a greater degree of interactive compliance.

The EPA interactive compliance program is broader than OSHA's in that it covers more programs and more regulatory issues. However, very few awards have been given out thus far, so it is hard to determine whether the impact of the award incentive will extend to many industries. The two federal agencies have evolved widely differing approaches to certification, with OSHA requiring formal applications and extensive proofs as a precondition to certification. The OSHA certification and recertification process is elaborate and costly to both business and government, but certified companies have obtained some rewards from closer working relationships with the agency. The EPA Region Six awards depend on substantial participation by state regulators and by business and environmental groups at the final stages of selection, whereas OSHA's Star Program does not require this kind of interaction.

EPA's Region Six plans to extend its excellence awards into other areas of environmental regulation. More significantly, the experiment seems to be appealing to other regions which may jump on the bandwagon in the future. The highly decentralized nature of the EPA encourages this kind of experimentation, and it is probable that EPA headquarters may adopt some features of Region Six's excellence program in the future. In terms of the theory of interactive compliance, this approach strongly resembles the certification procedure advocated by Sigler and Murphy in 1988. However, it is questionable whether such a program can be appealing to industry without greater incentives than public awards, pins, and flags. In a few years we shall be able to gauge the effectiveness of this bold experiment in environmental interactive compliance by observing the impact of the program on other industries in Region Six.

Whether interactive compliance can be extended to other areas of federal regulation may well depend on the experience gained with these two agency programs. Federal regulators are reluctant to depart from the strict enforcement activity that dominates regulatory policy. This reluctance stems from a fear that the agency will be seen as excessively lenient or probusiness. Furthermore, private suits by consumers, environmentalists, workers, shareholders, and other private stakeholders have been directed against agencies to prod them into more vigorous enforcement. Not surprisingly, this has made agency enforcement officials chary of interactive efforts. Until evidence accumulates that interactive compliance can improve compliance without compromise to the public interest, it will be difficult to persuade administrators to launch additional experiments. Even so, many enforcement officials are beginning to see the compliance benefits of corporate self-regulation, and there are many signs that corporations that have reliable self-regulation systems can expect recognition and reward. In this regard the Department of Defense has recognized government contractors that have such systems. Another chapter of this book describes the role of private auditing firms in establishing such systems.

The Mine Safety and Health Act of 1977 [30 U.S.C. secs. 801–23, 101 (c)] contains some elements that can encourage greater cooperation between the Mine Safety and Health Administration and regulated companies. The act allows the Secretary of Labor to modify mine safety standards if alternative methods are developed by mine owners. These alternative measures must afford miners the same level of protection provided by general standards, and each application must be approved by the agency. Under this statute almost 600 petitions for modifications have been granted.

Mine Safety and Health Administration regulations also permit mine owners to submit their own plans for such matters as dust control, roof support, and ventilation [30 C.F.R. sec. 70.1-90-301 (1981)]. This kind of regulatory flexibility is costly to the agency because of the expense of investigation and approval, but it encourages the industry to develop guidelines that are appropriate to specific mining conditions. This approach could be extended by statute to other areas of regulation in order to promote interactive compliance.

At the local level, County Administrator Lou Bezich ably describes in Chapter 5 an interactive compliance scheme for Camden County, New Jersey, health and food inspection activities. This program is an experiment in county certification of high-performance firms that have outstanding self-regulative programs to protect consumers.

There may be other state and local examples of interactive compliance in various programs around the country, but there appear to be very few of them. Apparently, state and local governments stimulate responsible corporate behavior almost entirely by threats and negative sanctions. In this setting, concealment and evasion are inadvertently encouraged. Those who are concerned with the development of decent and ethical standards of business conduct should want an expansion of interactive compliance so that ethical and lawful behavior could be enhanced. In a competitive marketplace it is difficult to maintain high standards of conduct when ethical firms might be economically disadvantaged by their policies. State and local governments can play a larger role in encouraging high standards of corporate conduct by recognizing and rewarding firms that exceed minimal standards. Moreover, the tone of business-government relationships can be changed from mutual mistrust to cooperation. Higher standards of corporate behavior can and will flourish in a culture of cooperation. Since so much of the responsibility for implementation of higher standards of conduct can be placed at the grass-roots level, much more experimentation with interactive compliance seems needed.

In 1979 the state of Florida adopted an Improved Home Energy Efficiency Code (Fla. Stat. sec. 553.901), which is a fine example of interactive compliance. Under this statute all new buildings erected in the state must meet minimum prescribed energy efficiency standards. At first there was considerable opposition to the code from building and construction groups, which complained that the code was too complex and unsuitable to the Florida climate. In response to these criticisms the state revised the residential compliance section of the home energy code to allow a certain latitude to builders in designing and constructing energy-efficient buildings, while retaining minimum envelope insulation and infiltration requirements and efficiency ratings for air conditioners, heat pumps, water heaters, and space heaters (Stanton 1986).

The key feature of Florida's revised Improved Home Energy Efficiency Code is its incentive approach, called the residential point system method. This method is based on an energy usage per square foot calculation. The code merely sets performance standards, but permits customized compliance according to "compliance budgets," which allow great flexibility in meeting overall compliance levels. Under the code, calculations of estimated annual heating and cooling requirements are set, but these are affected by the residential design, which creates different levels of air infiltration. In addition, builders receive credits for building homes incorporating the latest energy-saving technologies in hot water heating, space heating, and space cooling. This credit system allows builders to claim energy-efficient housing comparisons in sales to home purchasers, a form of certification under interactive compliance. The effect of the code is to encourage competition in the construction industry to exceed code standards for energy efficiency.

There are no specific penalties for noncompliance with the Improved Home Energy Efficiency Code. However, before a building permit can be issued, the prescribed energy efficiency form must be satisfactorily completed. Permitting remains a function of local government, but the Florida Department of Community Affairs provides code compliance forms to local building code offices and sells code books and instruction manuals to assist builders (Stanton 1986, 7). The state agency concentrates on positive incentives, rather than the threat of sanctions, to gain compliance.

Cooperation with Florida builders has been the cornerstone of the energy efficiency program. In revising the code the Florida Home Builders' Association received a grant from the governor's Energy Office to prepare a manual, a videotape, training seminars, and a brochure to encourage builders to respond to the flexible performance standards of the code. Code training is also the function of the Florida Department of Community Affairs, which gives one-day scheduled seminars and other training on request. Local building code officers have also needed training due to their unfamiliarity with code provisions (Stanton 1986, 8).

In California the Fairfield-Suisin Sewer District provides another innovative example of interactive compliance at the grass-roots level. The sewer district's contract for the operation and maintenance of its advanced wastewater treatment facility employs a unique public/private partnership incentive program, which rewards the private contractor for operation and maintenance excellence, cost reductions, and energy conservation. Such cost-cutting measures as neglect of maintenance are discouraged through carefully designed incentives. According to Richard F. Luthy, Jr., plant general manager/district engineer, the program has been refined and improved since its introduction in 1980 in order to respond to community needs and to the profit motive of private contractors.

The 1980 contract was the first in the nation to employ a performance incentive program for private operation of a public facility. Presently, the contract provides a performance-based incentive system that rewards the contractor on an annual basis for meeting objective performance standards specified each year in the contract. Meeting National Pollutant Discharge Elimination System (NPDES) permit compliance standards is worth 25 percent of the performance incentive pool. To earn the monthly incentive in this category, the contractor must meet or exceed NPDES permit requirements for ten different constituent elements. If two or more monthly elements are in noncompliance, 20 percent is deducted from the contractor's earnings in that category. Detailed provisions regarding monetary awards added to and penalties deducted from the performance pool are found in the contract provisions, based largely on NPDES standards.

However, 18 percent of the performance incentive pool is based on subjective performance criteria related to the goals, objectives, and expectations of the sewer district. At the beginning of each calendar quarter the district manager and the contractor meet to discuss how closely the contractor's performance is meeting the district's expectations. The payments from the performance incentive pool are made semiannually, based on the recommendations of the district manager (Luthy 1989).

Preventive maintenance also accounts for 25 percent of the performance incentive pool. To earn the monthly incentive in this category, the contractor must perform all scheduled preventive maintenance tasks. For each preventive maintenance scheduled frequency not achieved during a month the contractor loses 10 percent of the available monthly incentive in this category.

Funding for this program comes from sewer service charges and connection fees. To justify the contract, the public must be satisfied that the program has been effective. The district has achieved one of the best compliance records of any wastewater treatment plant in the United States, and its national and state awards provide substantial, objective evidence that private/public partnerships supported by cash incentives can be successful. The ingredients in this example that may help account for its acclaim include the following: (1) The incentives motivate private contractors to maintain excellence. (2) The performance criteria, which exceed minimum legal requirements, have spurred private contractors to perform at a high level. (3) The specificity of the contract, with its annual reconstruction, ensures the protection of the public and requires a close working relationship between the public and the private sectors.[1] According to Plant General Manager Luthy, monetary incentive programs are difficult to deal with in a political arena, and each year the sewer district must reclarify and justify the program to the public. This has been done since 1980. In 1986 the public approved, without federal or state assistance, a bond issue to improve and expand plant capacity (Luthy 1989).

Few other examples of local government experiments in interactive compliance provide such a dramatic success story. Plainly, this example could be extended to many other situations involving private contractors. Whether it would work as well with the general regulation of private industry is questionable. Direct monetary incentives may be the purest form of encouragement for compliance, but they are rarely available to regulators.

Nonetheless, the quest for examples of interactive compliance is potentially very fruitful. Much useful experience is being accumulated at the local levels of government. Communication of local successes is very limited, and examples are isolated and rarely known across the nation. The next step would seem to be a systematic collection of positive examples of interactive compliance in a working handbook that provides detailed information.

NOTE

1. Specifications for Contract Operations and Maintenance of District Wastewater Treatment Facilities, Fairfield County, 1989, pp. 1–29. This extensive document must be examined with care, especially pages twenty-eight through thirty, which provide the needed detail to permit micromanagement of potential pollution problems. Copies of specifications can be obtained from Fairfield County, California.

5

A County Experiment in Interactive Compliance

Louis S. Bezich

The Silver Platter Award is a pilot program in Camden County, New Jersey, that applies the theory of interactive corporate compliance. As of this writing, the program is completing full start-up, and, therefore, success cannot yet be measured; however, the program's design and development do offer what I believe is an informative look at this theory. Moreover, Camden County's experiment with interactive corporate compliance is especially important to the advancement of the theory because it is conducted by local government—a level of government that must begin to implement such theories if it is to be truly effective in changing government regulation in the United States.

The Silver Platter program contains the three basic elements necessary for its effectiveness: management commitment, education and awareness, and implementation and control. This voluntary program builds on the traditional regulatory function of restaurant inspection and provides business with an incentive to exceed state-mandated standards. In turn, the county government is provided with a means to increase compliance and reduce costs.

As I will describe, top management from a sample group of restaurant representatives has made a commitment to the program, and some managers have even volunteered to participate in county-sponsored training. Education and training have been built in as components of the program. Implementation and control have been accomplished by working closely with county food inspectors.

Under the program, full-service, for-profit restaurants in Camden County, known as Class I restaurants,* may, on a voluntary basis, join Silver Platter. To participate, a restaurant must meet two standards that it is not required to meet under the New Jersey Sanitary Code. First, it must send at least one employee each year to a county-administered food service training class. Second, it must conduct four quarterly self-inspections and complete a checklist prescribed by the county Division of Health.

If a participating restaurant has satisfied these two requirements and continues to meet all of the standards normally required for a Satisfactory rating under state law, along with all administrative requirements such as payment of fees, the restaurant will receive a Silver Platter Award from the Camden County Board of Freeholders (the governing body) and the Division of Health. The award is issued for one year and may be mentioned in advertisements and prominently displayed in the restaurant. The county will give the names of the award recipients to the press.

If at any time during the year of award the restaurant loses its Satisfactory rating, the award is withdrawn. Program literature stresses that "the award is based on sanitation criteria alone, and does not reflect aesthetic qualities, standards of service, menu, or price."

INCENTIVES FOR COUNTY GOVERNMENT

Why should Camden County undertake such a program? In 1989 there was only one case of food-borne illness that reached the level of an "outbreak," meaning an incidence of food-borne illness that involved two or more persons who ate common food, with the food confirmed as the source of the illness by a laboratory analysis.

On the financial side, the costs involved in instituting the program represent only a small portion of the county's total budget. So, then, where are the incentives for the county government?

Three factors support the Silver Platter program: cost savings, increased compliance, and development of a model for application elsewhere in county government.

Cost Saving

The Camden County Division of Health inspected 2,346 restaurants in 1989; of this number, 465, or approximately 20 percent, required

*Class I restaurants are full-service restaurants and do not include fast-food establishments or convenience stores.

at least one reinspection. The cost of an inspection or reinspection is about $150. An inspection is estimated to last two hours, on average, with travel.

Based on the 1989 volume, initial restaurant inspection cost Camden County over $350,000, with reinspection adding another $70,000. Of the reinspections, Class I restaurants, the subject of Silver Platter, accounted for 60 percent, or 280. This puts the cost of reinspection for Class I restaurants just over $40,000.

Fees are charged to restaurants for inspections and reinspections. In 1989, the fee for an initial inspection was $50, and for reinspection, $20. These fees were increased in 1990 to $75 and $35, respectively. Like many government user fees, the cost of the service is only partially underwritten by the fee.

Reconciling the revenue against gross costs, one can see that the net cost to the taxpayers for restaurant inspection in 1989 was over $234,000; for reinspection, just over $60,000; and for reinspection of Class I restaurants, just over $36,000. This assumes 100 percent collection of fees, which is not always the case.

A hard look at the numbers reveals that the net cost of reinspection of Class I restaurants is $36,000. However, it is important to recognize that Class I establishments represent a trial group, and the trial program, if successful, can provide a basis to expand Silver Platter to all facilities inspected. Therefore, any analysis of the potential savings in this class alone should be coupled with an understanding that a larger program value is involved.

Camden County's budget in 1989 was $189 million. Now, while restaurant inspection costs represent only a small portion of the total, they still offer the potential for savings. A 20 percent reduction in the cost of inspections would yield over $46,000, enough to provide housing for a homeless family or pay for an investigator for our county prosecutor's drug task force. If reinspections were cut in half, the county would save an additional $30,000 annually, enough to train several volunteer firefighters and/or add a counselor at a prenatal clinic. As I will discuss shortly, the changing nature of county government, in assuming more and more functions, adds value to the long-term potential of programs like Silver Platter.

Increased Compliance

The second goal of Silver Platter is increased compliance. As the figures above indicate, 20 percent of all inspections result in the need for a reinspection. Restaurant sanitation in New Jersey is required by the New Jersey Sanitary Code [N.J. Admin. Code secs. 8:24-1.1, 11.15 (1978)]. The code is part of an evolving body of laws and administrative regulations in New Jersey, beginning with the Local Health Services Act [N.J. Stat. Ann. secs. 26:3A2-2, 20 (1976)], passed in 1976. This law provides local (i.e., municipal) boards of health with the authority to enforce the code.

The code itself came into being in 1972 as part of an effort of the New Jersey Public Health Council to implement uniform standards and enforcement. The most recent state amendment to the code came in 1983. Changes are needed to create incentives.

Restaurant inspections yield three possible ratings: Satisfactory, Conditionally Satisfactory, and Unsatisfactory. Inspections are conducted at least once a year under the code. Conditionally Satisfactory and Unsatisfactory ratings require reinspection and could result in closure. A county certificate bearing the inspection rating must be prominently displayed in the restaurant. Typically, the newspapers serving Camden County publish the results of inspections, and some carry the detailed report written up by the inspectors.

Under the same body of law, counties in New Jersey have the option of establishing county boards of health or one of four administrative structures to implement regulatory policy. In 1967 Camden County created a health department, later to be reclassified as a division, and began entering into inter-local service agreements with its municipalities to act as the enforcing entity for health, including restaurant inspection. Since 1982, when the township of Cherry Hill entered the county system, the county Division of Health has acted as the enforcement agency for all municipalities in the county, with the county's public health officer acting as the municipal health officer.

In 1983 the county consolidated the financing of health functions within the county's property tax rate. Prior to 1983 the county had levied a separate health tax for the participating municipalities.

While there was only one case of confirmed food-borne illness in 1989, and a review of statistics shows that this is representative of the county's history, there is great interest in improving compliance beyond the cost savings.

First, it must be recognized that a confirmed outbreak of food-borne illness is not the most meaningful measure of the Health Division's regulatory performance. As was noted, a full 20 percent of all inspections require reinspections. One need not leap to the level of an outbreak to conclude that the public health mission of the government could be improved by a decrease in the number of required reinspections.

If anything, a single case of food-borne illness can reflect negatively on the regulators (i.e., the county) as well as the establishments. As in any regulatory relationship, a problem will bring cries for stricter enforcement and inquiries as to the quality of current enforcement. In sum, there is always a need to increase compliance.

Second, the tougher standards in Silver Platter's self-inspection program are based on standards that may become mandatory in years to come. Inclusion of such standards now begins to move Camden County establishments in the right direction which will make enforcement much easier if such standards do become mandatory.

Known as the Hazard Analysis Critical Control Point (HACCP), these standards currently exceed those used in annual inspections. The state of New Jersey is currently studying the possibility of extending HACCP to the New Jersey Sanitary Code. Silver Platter will offer a model to test the effects of such standards and the impact they can have on sanitation.

Counties as Laboratories of Democracy

Finally, Silver Platter's greatest impact will come from its application to other regulatory functions. County government is being looked to more and more as a regional provider of public services. State governments and municipalities see the economies of scale offered by counties and see county government as the answer to their problems.

For example, here in Camden County we have taken on many responsibilities previously within the domain of municipalities: police and fire dispatch, solid waste disposal, sewage treatment, and police training.

As the new "laboratories of democracy," county governments will need to avail themselves of every innovation. Interactive corporate compliance is certainly one to apply.

BUSINESS INCENTIVES

Why should business get involved in Silver Platter? The annual ritual of the board of health inspection is unpleasant and worrisome enough; why should restaurants embrace such a concept? Simply put, it is good for business.

The Silver Platter program offers a low-cost, easily administered process that can preempt sanitation problems and generate some positive publicity. Reputation is the lifeblood of restaurants. In fact, a number of restaurant industry publications have identified reputation as one of the most important factors in the selection of a restaurant.

A sanitation problem can push a business into bankruptcy. One failed inspection, one case of food-borne illness, or one negative newspaper article can spell doom. The restaurant industry takes sanitation seriously since it can have a direct impact on profits. There is an inherent incentive to seek high levels of compliance.

Conversely, an award for sanitation can enhance a restaurant's reputation. Knowing that an establishment not only meets, but also exceeds minimum standards can provide patrons with a great deal of comfort.

Finally, legal liability is another incentive for a restaurant to do as much as possible to maintain a high level of compliance. According to the National Institute for the Foodservice Industry, the Uniform Commercial Code provides an option to people who want compensation for illness or injury resulting from unsafe food products. People suing need only prove that the food was unfit, that it caused them harm, and that in serving them unfit food the operator violated the warranty of sale.

PROGRAM DEVELOPMENT

Camden County's development of the Silver Platter program provides some insight into all of the elements of regulatory reform described by Jay A. Sigler and Joseph E. Murphy. Application of the theory was prompted by my interest in the concept as well as by my practical need as Camden County administrator to find ways to save money and improve services wherever possible.

More specifically, the choice of restaurant inspection was based on (1) the ability to easily grasp the purpose and procedures of restaurant inspection; (2) the county's control over the inspection process—we employ the inspectors and issue the ratings; (3) the county's legal ability to establish Silver Platter by a simple resolution of the board of freeholders—no approval by any other level of government was necessary; (4) a determination that the restaurant community could engage in the program without any major costs; (5) the extremely low cost to the county government, which would generate a net savings to the taxpayers; and (6) the notion that the county could adopt criteria that would create a new classification beyond the statutorily defined ratings, which focused on excellence, rather than minimum standards. Coupled with this was the notion that we would prevail on the newspapers to publish the award winners—a fitting act, given the years of publishing dry inspection reports.

Camden County is governed by a board of freeholders: seven officials elected at large for three-year, staggered terms. The terms are staggered such that at least one and usually two terms expire each year, resulting in a freeholder election every year.

Our government can be described as a commission or noncharter form. Each of the freeholders is assigned responsibility for an area of the government through a committee chairmanship. The freeholders engage in both legislative and executive functions.

The freeholders are considered part-time officials and appoint a full-time professional, the county administrator, to run the affairs of the government on a day-to-day basis. Each area of freeholder responsibility is normally headed by a department director who has a dual reporting responsibility—reporting both to the freeholder in charge of his or her area and to the county administrator.

The level of involvement of freeholders varies depending on the individual. By law, a freeholder may become involved to whatever level of administrative detail he or she wishes. Conversely, a freeholder may delegate administrative responsibility to the administrator, choosing to focus on broader policy matters. The relationship among the freeholders, county administrator, and department heads is primarily a product of personality and operating style.

Each January the board of freeholders elects a freeholder-director from among its ranks. The director chairs meetings of the board, recommends committee assignments, and often represents the position of the board.

When embarking on the application of interactive corporate compliance, I utilized an inside-out approach. I first sought support from within the county political and administrative structure and then presented it to the restaurant community.

Selling the Concept to the Board of Freeholders

First, I discussed the concept with my freeholder-director. The freeholder-director in Camden County is both a governmental and a political leader. His support is crucial to the advancement of the policy agenda, and in this case the director supported the Silver Platter program.

Next came the freeholder in charge of the Health Division. It was important to get his support for both governmental and political reasons. Governmentally, his support was necessary if the concept was to advance procedurally; as a freeholder-in-charge, he holds an informal veto power over the program. Politically, the freeholder is a member of the minority party and is one of the most vocal members of the minority. His support would ensure bipartisan consensus of the two key elected officials, support that will be necessary as the program unfolds. The freeholder-in-charge also supported the proposal.

Bipartisan support would remove any opposition down the line so as to eliminate Silver Platter as a bargaining chip or means of leverage in any political contest. This early support was sustained by reporting regularly on program development and including the freeholders in program-related events.

Selling the Concept to the Division of Health

I then discussed the matter with the staff from the Department of Health and Human Services, which includes the Division of Health. Using the wherewithal of my office and the added support of the two freeholders, I outlined the goals and nature of the program.

Staff was generally receptive to the idea, but clearly this was because of the level of managerial and political commitment. It was apparent from the outset that my proposal for applying the theory of interactive corporate compliance to the restaurant function was viewed as "more work" and something outside the norm.

One of the first moves of the department director was to link Silver Platter to his goal of automating the inspection report process. He viewed the program as a means to ensure support for the purchase of laptop computers with which inspectors could prepare reports more quickly and in a standard fashion. This, he advocated, would make the reports (which are often published), and particularly the language of the reports, less subject to the individual styles of the inspectors.

One means by which I ensured the development of the proposal was through the assignment of a graduate student intern from my office. This energetic intern carried the ball through the early days of the program. Through the intern I was able to control the development, mainly seeing that the proposal moved forward consistent with the theory.

Development initially moved slowly. Health Division staff tied up my intern in a series of meetings, paper shuffling, and normal bureaucratic delays. Division staff always responded, albeit somewhat slowly, but never let themselves get into a set of circumstances when they could be criticized for not being responsive. I draw a distinction between embracing the concept and taking a proactive approach to the project, and being sufficiently responsive to a directive from the administrator's office.

Adding to the slow pace were my schedule constraints. Because this was a special project of my office, Health Division staff often wanted my time to review program materials. While the intern was helpful, ultimately decisions had to be made, and I was looked to for those decisions.

Nevertheless, development moved forward. After several drafts and almost nine months, the final criteria and award system were ready. At this stage I reported on the progress of the program to the two freeholders. Again, they were both supportive.

It is important to note that after the fifth month of development, the graduate intern finished her stay with the government. At that juncture I pointed out to the Health Division staff that they were charged with responsibility for seeing to the final development and implementation of the program. This transfer of responsibility and change of duty was, in my judgment, an important milestone. Division staff members were now going to be held directly accountable for the success of the program. This was no longer a special project of the administrator's office, but an integral part of their list of assignments.

Another important milestone occurred during the development of the program: A new director for the Department of Health and Human Services was appointed by the Board of Freeholders. One of the tasks of the new department director, as articulated by me, was to step up the development of Silver Platter. I was becoming disturbed with the length of time things were taking and what I believed was a casual attitude toward the program. With this directive the program moved at a more rapid pace.

Selling the Concept to the Restaurant Industry

It was now time for my office to take the program to the restaurant industry and to get back into the marketing of the program. Specifically, the division's Silver Platter program coordinator and I met with representatives of five restaurants. The purpose of the meetings was twofold: (1) to explain the program and get feedback on its design and (2) to solicit support. To kick off the program, we planned to invite representatives of the 350-plus Class I restaurants to a program briefing. Prior to the briefing, however, I wanted to "test the waters" and create some allies among the ranks of the industry. These preliminary meetings, as I will describe shortly, were successful. We learned a lot, picked up some allies, and polished up our product.

Selling the Concept to the Inspectors

To this point, I had had no personal contact with any of the inspectors. While the program had been explained to them by management at the division, they had not heard from top management. To remedy this, I met with a group of five inspectors.

At the meeting I explained the nature and purpose of the program and how important they were to the success of Silver Platter. I showed them the brochures and discussed my meeting with the restaurants. Most importantly, I gave them the opportunity to ask questions and discuss their concerns. The meeting went well. Their concerns were reasonable and reflected the seriousness with which they viewed the program. In the next section I provide the details of the meeting.

Selling the Concept to the New Jersey Department of Health

One final actor with an interest in our agenda is the New Jersey Department of Health. Division staff have reviewed the program with the state officials, who have expressed support. Use of the HACCP standards is key here. The view among health officials is that the HACCP standards are the next step in advancing the public health agenda as it applies to restaurant sanitation. Developing a pilot program in Camden County where HACCP can be tested on a voluntary basis—and, moreover, where restaurants will be rewarded for voluntary compliance—provides a model for statewide application. Certainly, Camden County is pleased to provide such a model program and will enjoy the state support. In an era when many states and counties are working at cross purposes, we are pleased that our gesture to involve the state in our program was so well received.

THE PROGRAM COMPONENTS

The Criteria

The first task was to develop criteria that gave the county a basis on which to recognize excellent performance, while not being obstructive and while building on the existing practices. Health Division staff recommended the HACCP self-inspection checklist and the annual training requirement.

As I have already noted, the HACCP standards exceed those currently set out in the New Jersey Sanitary Code, thus making compliance with such higher standards worthy of recognition. In addition, the HACCP standards are specific, in place, and reduced to checklist format.

Under the Silver Platter the division will mail self-inspection checklists to program participants four times each year. The checklists must be completed, signed, and dated. They must be maintained in the restaurant's files and be available for inspection by the Health Division's inspector during the regular annual inspection.

If at least one quarterly inspection report has been completed and is on file, then the self-inspection criteria have been satisfied. I hasten to note that the number of self-inspection reports required will increase in the second year of the program. The one-report benchmark represents a first-year start-up requirement.

Participants will be briefed by division personnel on the nature and use of the checklist as a self-assessment tool at the general briefing as well as during the annual inspections. It is envisioned that division inspectors will use the checklist as an educational tool during inspections.

The second standard recommended by the division related to training. The Camden County Health Division regularly conducts food handling courses, which are open to any interested party. One municipality in the county, the township of Cherry Hill, requires all restaurants in the township to send staff to these training courses. Outside of this local mandate, no government incentive is offered for attendance. Under Silver Platter, such incentives would be offered.

The second standard is consistent with what Sigler and Murphy have espoused and, more directly, with what has been a prominent theme among health professionals. The fit here is especially good.

Under the Silver Platter program each participating restaurant must send at least one employee to at least one class each year. Classes normally last eight hours and are administered in one- or two-day sessions. Given throughout the year, classes cover such topics as proper food holding temperatures, proper food preparation, and bacteriology and personal hygiene. Classes may be scheduled in county facilities or on site at a restaurant facility.

One particularly exciting element of the education component is the potential for direct interactive involvement of the restaurants in training. Acting as guest lecturers or serving on industry panels, representatives from the restaurant industry can become directly involved in this educational effort.

It is estimated that completing the quarterly self-inspections should take 30 to 40 minutes depending on the size of the facility. Training involves a greater allocation of staff time, but can generate rewards commensurate with the investment.

Legal review of the criteria yielded no problems. Technically, the board of freeholders is creating its own award for establishments that meet the criteria established by the same board. The standards are in addition to and not in place of the standards legally prescribed by the New Jersey Sanitary Code.

The Award

Some discussion about the award itself is appropriate since it is one of the motivating factors in the program. Exhibit 1 shows the Silver Platter. It has been designed and named for use in advertising.

The original program brochure intentionally contains a rendering of the plaque so that restaurant operators can see exactly what they will get. When I conducted my preliminary meetings with selected industry representatives, I not only showed them a rendering of the award, but also provided them with a mock-up of a telephone directory ad that included the Silver Platter Award (see Exhibit 2).

Exhibit 1
The Silver Platter Award

Exhibit 2
Advertisements Highlighting the Silver Platter Award

Special emphasis was placed on the invitation to this industry briefing. A conscientious effort was made not to have the invitation look like something issued by a government. Rather, it was designed as a marketing tool that would be used to capture the attention of our potential customers with whom we wished to enhance our business relationship.

The Camden County area presently has two awards that are given to restaurants among other establishments: *Philadelphia Magazine*'s Best of Philadelphia award and the *Courier-Post* newspaper's Best of South Jersey award. Winners often reference these awards in their advertisements and display the award itself prominently in their restaurant.

Our goal is to replicate and indeed exceed the interest in these awards through the Silver Platter program. Silver Platter's basis in government and sanitation makes it a complement to these other award programs. The reception given these two awards, particularly in the restaurant industry, suggests that Silver Platter may be equally well received.

ANALYSIS

Thus far, I have described how Camden County has applied the theory of interactive corporate compliance to our restaurant inspection function, the basis for selecting restaurant inspection as the area in which to experiment, and the incentives to both the county government and the restaurant industry. In my description I have demonstrated how the Camden County model contains the elements necessary for a successful interactive corporate compliance program as set forth by Sigler and Murphy: management commitment, education and awareness, and implementation and control.

At this point it is appropriate to examine in greater detail the motivations and actions of the players in the process. This will provide further insight into the model, as well as shedding light on the implementation of the theory.

The Board of Freeholders

Like most governing bodies, the Camden County Board of Freeholders will be supportive of the Silver Platter program so long as it meets its goals without a major disruption in the restaurant industry. As with any policy issue, success will be contingent on control of any interest groups that may have an agenda adverse to the goals of the program. This is precisely why the restaurant community has been approached early on. Ongoing success will be contingent on sustaining a good relationship and satisfying any opposing voices.

The success of the program must be translated into political and governmental terms. There need to be specific examples or demonstrations of "how things are better" because of the program.

Positive publicity, policy forums with government and industry representatives, and success stories that make people feel good about dining out in Camden County must occur if the program is to grow and flourish. In the words of Sigler and Murphy, the program must meet the test of a practical, results-oriented analysis.

As a matter of governmental and political reality, the program must also demonstrate a savings to the taxpayer, something that the freeholders can point to with pride. While these points may seem obvious to students of politics, I believe they are extremely important to reiterate. Application of interactive corporate compliance in a large federal regulatory environment may prove successful if those who are directly involved and knowledgeable are functioning without generating major controversy. The range between day-to-day implementation and policy-making authority is not so wide in local government, and the bureaucratic or institutional cushion that can provide time and flexibility to engage in such experiments does not exist there. I offer this observation as a comment on the environmental constraints on innovation in local government and as a means of adding some context for the need to place extra attention on such factors in local applications of interactive corporate compliance.

It is my opinion, one that I readily admit is biased, that if applications of such theories as interactive corporate compliance can meet what I believe is the more stringent test of local government application, then they will have a far greater chance of being used as a tool for regulatory reform throughout the United States.

The Restaurant Industry

The preliminary meeting with selected representatives from the restaurant industry proved helpful and encouraging. As I noted earlier, the Silver Platter coordinator and I met with a sample of operators to test the concept and receive input. The group included representatives of a single-family-owned restaurant, a national chain, a hotel restaurant, an ethnic restaurant, and a small restaurant operated by a corporation. All of these representatives could be considered top management in their respective organizations.

It was clear in the discussions that the majority of the operators would be receptive because we were from the Health Division and there was no desire whatsoever to do anything that would cause us to be unhappy or that would otherwise impact on their rating. While not overly prominent, there was a clear sense that the regulators should be listened to.

In order to allay the concerns of some of the industry representatives, I placed special emphasis on the business incentives provided by the program. My goal was to get management commitment based on the merits of the program, rather than out of concern about their basic relationship with the Health Division.

As we explained the voluntary nature of the program and the incentives, the reactions unfolded. The larger chains were enthusiastic because many were already conducting some of the same internal inspections. Some agreed to participate in industry panels as part of the training program. However, few agreed to share specific inspection checklists because they considered the information to be proprietary and not to be disseminated in the interest of fair competition. Similarly, the larger chains welcomed training since this was already part of their internal control and staff development program.

Some operators felt that Silver Platter would mean unfair competition since establishments that choose not to join or that are unable to join would be looked at unfavorably by their patrons. Choosing not to join does not mean that a restaurant is unsanitary; it will still be subject to the same annual inspection guidelines and rating criteria under the law. But by establishing Silver Platter as an optional program and recognizing those who meet the tougher standards, some suggested the freeholders would be unfairly penalizing those who meet all the existing regulations.

Still others saw merit in any process that would support improved working relationships between government and business and, in particular, improved sanitation.

The bottom line with most operators was that the criteria were not unreasonable, costly, or grossly unfair. The true test will no doubt come at the general briefing and throughout implementation. Thus far, there is a basis on which to move forward.

Division Staff and Management

The inspectors were quick to tell me and division management that Silver Platter would place more stress on them. They said there would by "much more riding" on their annual inspection with the prospect of a Silver Platter Award. Other questions and comments focused on the procedures under the program, the commitment of top management, and, of course, the status of the laptop computers.

After expressing my support for the use of computers (which I believe *is* a good idea separate from the program) and the expediting of their purchase, I confronted the stress issue. Simply put, it was my opinion that the program would reduce stress and make their job easier. I explained the nature and purpose of the program and the specific goal of eliminating the adversarial relationship that often existed, particularly in restaurant inspection.

The inspectors understood the program thoroughly and were most concerned with management's support of their work, should there be any problem implementing the new program. I expressed my support and discussed the basis of their feelings.

All in all, the session went well, with a lot of "clear the air" type comments being made by both labor and management. Above all, I explained how I saw the success of the program as hinging on their attitude and enthusiasm for Silver Platter, specifically pointing out that I would be willing to recommend merit salary adjustments for inspectors whose performance was exemplary in the development of Silver Platter.

The response of front-line personnel was not surprising. As with any new endeavor, they were concerned about the program's impact on them and what incentives would be available, if any, for outstanding performance. My responses were consistent with what I would recommend in any new program since support and rewards, in my judgment, must be built into any successful program. I would suggest that attention to front-line personnel is extremely critical to any application of interactive corporate compliance.

Many of the points regarding front-line personnel apply to management as well. Reasonable incentives and a "share of the business" so that managers feel committed are of equal necessity. Providing opportunities within the professional ranks and simple recognition are items that must be considered with professional staff.

As we approach program start-up, management has increased its commitment and is taking the lead role in implementation.

CONCLUSION

Whether Camden County's experiment with interactive corporate compliance proves successful remains to be seen. Thus far, the development of the Silver Platter Award has exhibited all the characteristics normally attributed to the creation of new government programs (i.e., sensitivity to politics, interest groups, and the implementing bureaucracy). The program's requirements and rewards have been purposely kept simple and straightforward so that the results can be easily measured. Positive rewards have been constructed, and a target audience has been identified. We have indications that top management will be committed to the program, and we have built in a requirement for education and training. Furthermore, I have suggested that Silver Platter's setting in county government exposes it to greater scrutiny and more immediate evaluation than that normally found in a federal setting.

All this is to say that the fundamental principles underlying the theory will undergo a true test if, as we have tried to do, they are applied wisely. As in any business relationship, the greater the risk, the greater the reward. I would suggest that the increased risks inherent in a local government application likewise offer the potential for greater rewards, inasmuch as there are literally thousands of local governments—counties, cities, special authorities, school districts—across this nation. If interactive corporate compliance represents a means of regulatory reform, then its success must be measured at all levels of government that perform regulatory functions.

6

Demonstrating Ethical Responsibility: Implementing a Self-Governance Program

Paul M. Carren and Richard B. Pazornik

> A long habit of not thinking a thing wrong gives it the superficial appearance of being right.
>
> Thomas Paine

Over the past decade, media and regulatory attention has focused time and time again on what has been perceived as corporate irresponsibility. No industry has escaped criticism of its ethical probity. Areas of business activity as diverse as the environment (Exxon Valdez), securities (Drexel Burnham Lambert), government procurement (Operation "Ill Wind"), and banking (Lincoln Savings) provide a few examples where corporate America has seemingly failed to uphold its responsibility to society at large, its customers, and its employees.

This chapter is intended to assist companies that either are developing a self-governance program or are already operating under some form of self-governance program and wish to reevaluate or update the program in light of the current environment. After reading this chapter, one will be able to identify the key elements of a successful self-governance program and to set a company agenda for implementing such a program.

In the past it was taken for granted that companies, like individuals, should act within the bounds of the law. The U.S. business community assumed that as long as an action was legal, it was condoned. One need not look too far in the past to see examples of this. For instance, it was legal for a restaurant to refuse to serve blacks or other minorities. It was legal for companies to discharge manufacturing byproducts and other pollutants into our air and waters. While these actions may have been legal, at no time were they moral or ethical. Since the late 1950s these practices have begun to change, as a result of both our heightened ethical awareness and our changing laws. Restaurants open to the public cannot refuse to serve black patrons, nor can companies wantonly pollute our air and waterways. Our laws set minimum standards; our ethics dictate our achievements. For example, during the 1980s there was a rash of product tamperings; one of the most infamous of these instances involved the product Tylenol. When the tamperings became known, the manufacturer, Johnson & Johnson, ordered all Tylenol removed from retail shelves in order to eliminate any potential consumer injury. This action cost Johnson & Johnson millions of dollars in lost revenues. While the manufacturer was not legally required to remove the product, its corporate ethics dictated this action. In the long run the benefits the company received both monetarily and in terms of its reputation have made the actions worthwhile.

CORPORATE RESPONSIBILITY . . . TO WHOM?

The operation of any business, large or small, entails the assumption of significant responsibilities. Not only is the business responsible to the owners to try to produce a fair profit, but also it is responsible to many other groups. As shown in Exhibit 3, these groups include

- employees
- customers
- vendors/suppliers
- community/society
- government

The responsibilities to each group differ; yet each is significant. These specific responsibilities should be embodied within a company's standard operating policies and procedures.

As early as 1919 companies began putting in writing what was expected of their employees and vendors and what could be expected of the organization. George Verity, founder of the American Rolling Mill Co. (now known as ARMCO, Inc.), penned his company's corporate standard of conduct. In addition to outlining the company's mission, the code stated how business should be conducted, what is

Exhibit 3
Organizational Responsibilities

expected of employees, what the organization owes to the employees, and the relationship to be fostered with customers. This code is still the model used today at ARMCO, Inc.

Employees

A company's employees are its most valuable asset. It is the employees who deal with customers, vendors, and the community at large. Even when employees are not at work, they may be seen as emissaries of the business organization. Most employees want to be dealt with fairly, and they want to be perceived as being valuable to the company. This value can be demonstrated in many ways, including developing challenges for employees, showing trust by the organization, and helping employees develop their potential. Salary, benefits, and conditions must also be reasonable in light of the work done. The company must provide an atmosphere in which employees may achieve company goals without being placed in ethical dilemmas. Furthermore, employees deserve fair treatment in both good and bad economic times. In return, employees owe the company their best efforts to achieve the organization's goals. Employees must strive to deliver quality products (goods or services) to customers (either external or internal to the organization).

Customers

To its customers a company has the responsibility to provide a quality product at a reasonable price. In addition, a company must treat its customers honestly, fairly, with respect and dignity, and at all times with courtesy. Even if a company is a sole-source producer, these responsibilities still exist. When a customer perceives there is a problem with a product, then that customer has a problem. The problem should be dealt with in a manner that is equitable to both the customer and the company.

Vendors/Suppliers

The company should pay its vendors/suppliers within the terms of the company's obligations. For example, if a contract provides for a prompt-payment discount, a company should take the discount only if payment is made within the terms. In return for dealing fairly with its vendors, a company should expect that its vendors will supply quality products in a timely manner at a reasonable price. Depending on the circumstances of a given situation, a company may find itself as either customer or vendor. Therefore, the company must, through its employees, act as it desires its vendors or customers to act.

Community/Society

Just like other citizens the corporate citizen has certain obligations to the community in which it operates. The company should set an example by its own actions. For example, IBM has a program that allows employees to take paid sabbaticals, during which employees teach at local institutions. This affords individuals the opportunity to do something ordinarily outside their reach and, at the same time, allows the company to help prepare competent individuals to enter the job market. Companies must be seen as promoting civic pride.

Government Contractors

For the government contractor it is even more important to understand the responsibilities to these groups. Government contractors perform under contracts that are financed with public funds. Consequently, they have a responsibility that requires that they ensure their performance is in compliance not only with contractual terms, but also with governing laws and regulations. Hence, it is extremely important that government contractor executives, management-level personnel, and other employees know and understand their roles and responsibilities in order to ensure compliance. This is usually accomplished by means of a self-governance program.

DEVELOPING STANDARDS OF CONDUCT

What Should Be Included in Standards of Conduct?

Standards of conduct serve as the backbone of any corporate self-governance program. These standards of conduct explain the company's mission, its obligations, and its expectations. The company's mission statement should be developed by the organization's executives. It should be clear in focus and aimed at giving an immediate understanding of the value the organization places on its customers, employees, vendors, and the community. For example, one Fortune 500 aerospace and electronics company's mission statement reads: "The corporation's basic objective is to conduct its business to benefit our customers, shareholders, employees, suppliers, and society in general. We seek to achieve our goals of profitability and growth while fulfilling the responsibilities of a corporate citizen."

In addition to the mission statement, the standards of conduct must also incorporate how the company expects its employees to act with respect to each other, vendors, and customers. Each statement should be clear and should speak directly to its target. For example, many companies prohibit employees from giving gifts to or receiving gifts from vendors. Thus, an appropriate statement might read as follows:

> Good business relationships are based on trust and providing quality products at reasonable prices. Toward that end, ABC Corp. believes that it is improper for its employees to give or receive gifts of whatever kind and value from its vendors/suppliers. The giving of such gifts, while not necessarily intended to influence buying activities may do so and could hinder employees from exercising their obligations effectively. Consequently, ABC Corp. believes that it is also improper for employees to give vendors and/or customers gifts of whatever nature, value or kind.

Who Should Implement the Standards of Conduct?

As part of an overall self-governance program, company standards of conduct must be implemented throughout the organization. Top-level management must be the loudest, strongest, and most sincere supporters of the standards of conduct. If midlevel management and line employees perceive a lack of commitment, the standards will be nothing more than "dressing." Management must be willing to live by the standards and ensure that the company's way of doing business is in line with the spirit of the standards before they can expect the rest of the organization to do likewise. In order to be successful, implementation must be from the top down, with each lower tier of employees accepting the standards as their own and making a commitment to themselves and to their coworkers to accept and enforce the standards.

There are many different self-governance models that companies may adapt to their particular needs. However, close examination of alternative approaches shows that they contain similar elements, regardless of the industry(ies) in which a company is involved or the company's size.

Management must realize at the outset that their company's most important asset is its employees. Furthermore, it is the company's employees who will face the daily ethical challenges of the marketplace. A company's investment in its self-governance program will be significant, both in terms of actual dollars invested and employee time. It is indeed an investment, however, and management must always set the example and become the most stalwart supporters of the company's self-governance program. Management must lead not only by their words, but also, more importantly, by their deeds. They must be willing to take positions on company matters that are ethically proper, yet might yield smaller short-term profits.

The federal government has long been a strong proponent of the theory that industry needs to adopt solid self-governance programs. The Department of Defense (DoD), the Securities and Exchange Commission (SEC), and the Occupational Safety and Health Administration (OSHA) all encourage companies to develop strong, effective self-governance programs. In addition to the government, many professional societies and civic organizations have adopted codes of ethics to assist their members in conducting their activities in an ethical manner.

Leading companies in the defense industry, partially as a result of the report by the Packard Commission (President's Blue Ribbon Commission on Defense Management, 1986), gathered together and developed a program that has become known as the Defense Industry

Initiatives (DII). The DII speak directly to the topic of industry self-governance and set standards for signatory companies against which they develop their self-governance programs. (Currently forty-eight companies have signed the DII.) The DII set forth six principles that, with slight modifications and additions, form the basis for a sound self-governance program, irrespective of the industry in which a company operates. These six principles are summarized as follows:

1. Every company should adhere to a written code of business ethics and conduct.
2. The company will train its employees concerning their personal responsibilities under the code.
3. The company will create an atmosphere that encourages employees to report violations of its code to the company without fear of retribution for such reporting.
4. Each company has the obligation to adopt procedures for voluntary disclosure of violations of laws and corrective actions taken.
5. Each company has a responsibility to live by standards of conduct that preserve the integrity of the defense industry.
6. Each company must be accountable for its commitment to these principles.

What Is the Benefit of Implementing a Self-Governance Program?

The implementation of a self-governance program provides many benefits to an organization. First, industry commitment to self-governance should decrease the need for the government to mandate what it believes to be appropriate and ethical contractor behavior.

During the Reagan presidency, Secretary of Defense Frank Carlucci wanted to require that virtually all defense contractors have a specific self-governance program, the components of which were to be mandated via the Defense Federal Acquisition Regulation. The mandating of self-governance would have given the government even more oversight responsibility and an even greater ability to intrude on individual companies.

Publicizing self-governance programs can provide immeasurable good will within the community and can influence the public's attitude toward a company in a positive manner. Further, if employees believe the program will be effective, they may begin to operate with a renewed spirit of camaraderie. In addition, by having an ongoing, viable program, companies may be able to avoid severe legal penalties if they can show that they have taken it on themselves to correct a problem, including disciplining violators as appropriate.

ELEMENTS OF A CORPORATE SELF-GOVERNANCE PROGRAM

When developing company standards of conduct, managers must ask themselves what the driving forces behind the company are and what the company's responsibilities to its customers, suppliers, employees, community, and owners are. The earning of short-term profits should not be the sole driving force, although it is appropriate as one of many goals. Indeed, where short-term profit is the sole driving force, unethical conduct may be the outcome. At times it is this emphasis that places employees and vendors in positions where ethical dilemmas are likely to be encountered. To determine a company's driving force, management most often confronts issues it has shied away from in the past. It is precisely those problems that must be addressed when a self-governance program is implemented.

Once a company has been identified as acting unethically, it is too late. Irreversible damage has already been done to the company's image. The harder the times are, the easier it is for employees to rationalize unethical behavior. That is when it is imperative for management to take a stand promoting ethical behavior. For example, in the Exxon Valdez incident in which an oil tanker ran aground, spilling millions of gallons of oil on the Alaskan shoreline, Exxon was considered by the public to be at fault for the spill and therefore responsible for the cleanup. However, in October of 1989, the company announced it was suspending cleanup operations. Had Exxon acted in an ethical manner?

We have taken the six principles noted above and adapted them for overall industry application:

1. The company will have a written code of business ethics and conduct.
2. The company will train all employees concerning their personal responsibilities under the code and will make known to vendors and customers the standards to which the company holds its employees.
3. The company will create an environment where employees and other persons feel free to report suspected violations of the code without fear of retribution by the organization. Upon receiving a report, the company will promptly investigate all suspected violations of the code.
4. Should violations be found, the company will promptly report the violations to the proper company officials for immediate internal correction and/or disciplinary action.
5. Should violations also violate local, state, of federal laws, appropriate disclosure will be made to the proper government authorities.

6. The program should be reviewed periodically to ensure that employees comprehend the full nature of the program and to renew top-level management commitment to the program.
7. The company should obtain an independent third-party review of the overall operation of the program.

These seven key elements, each important to the overall functioning of a viable self-governance program, are described in detail to assist with the development of efforts focused on the successful implementation of a self-governance program. These elements and their interrelationships can be expressed by the self-governance model shown in Exhibit 4.

Exhibit 4
Self-Governance Model

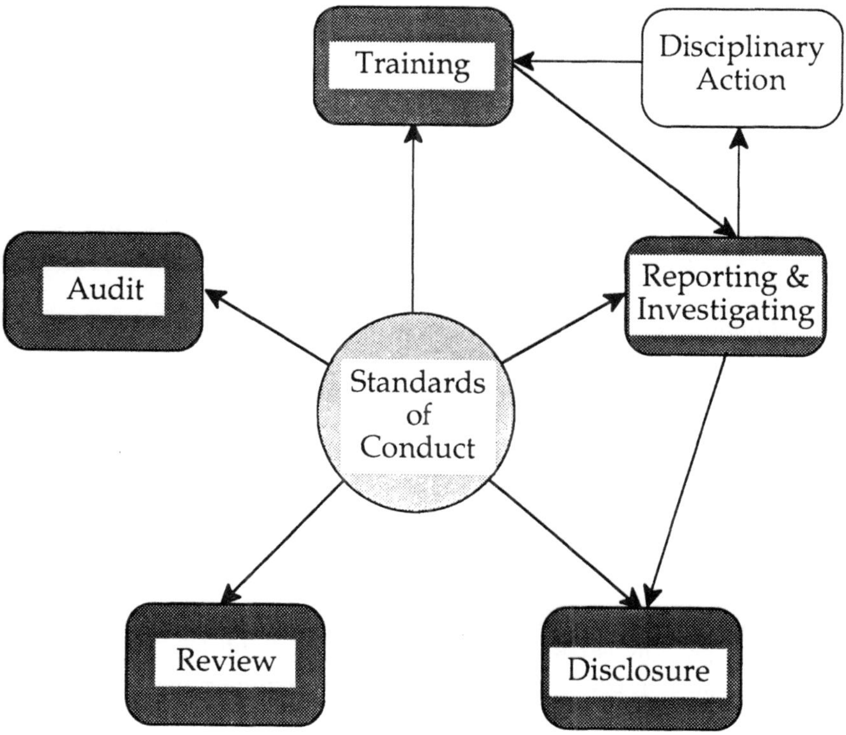

A Written Code of Business Ethics and Conduct

As stated earlier, the code of conduct is the cornerstone of a company's self-governance program. The code itself should be divided into several easy-to-understand sections. The first section should be the company's mission statement, which should come from the highest levels within the company and embody the basic philosophies of the organization. Foremost in this statement must be the strong commitment of the entire organization to integrity. The code must address all levels of the organization, from the CEO to the line worker. Each employee must know what is expected of him or her and what can be expected from the company. The code should also detail how the company will deal with customers, vendors, and the community. The statements that follow illustrate some of the ideas that might be appropriate for each group.

> *Customers*
>
> ABC Corp. will provide its customers, either public or private, with the highest-quality products and services on schedule and at reasonable prices.
>
> *Vendors*
>
> ABC Corp. will deal honestly and fairly with its vendors. All qualified vendors will receive fair consideration. Buying decisions will be based on overall value offered, which includes price, quality, and integrity of the vendor.
>
> *Employees*
>
> ABC Corp. is committed to providing a safe workplace for all employees. The working environment should be conducive to open communications between all employees and among all levels. ABC Corp. is committed to all equal employment practices. All employee relations are based on mutual trust, respect, and the dignity of every employee. ABC Corp. will provide its employees with competitive pay and benefits.
>
> *Community*
>
> ABC Corp. is committed to uphold all laws and regulations of the jurisdictions in which it conducts business. In addition, ABC Corp. believes it is the corporation's responsibility to support the local communities in which it operates. ABC Corp. is committed to protecting the environment and will not knowingly undertake any action that will cause harm to either the air or the waterways.
>
> *Government*
>
> ABC Corp. in its dealings with the government, must uphold the public trust that is part of undertaking a government contract. All

> employees who work on government contracts have a special responsibility to ensure that only properly chargeable costs are billed to or reimbursed by the government and that negotiations with the government are based on the Truth in Negotiations Act. Furthermore, it is incumbent on ABC Corp.'s employees to ensure the accuracy of all documents and certificates submitted to the government.

In addition to specifying responsibilities of the organization, the code should spell out what to do if a violation is suspected, including the alternatives available for reporting violations. A program may have several alternatives from which an employee may choose when reporting a suspected violation. One route might be having a private conference with the employee's supervisor. Another route might be reporting the matter to the department or division head. Still another might be reporting to the person designated by the organization to investigate suspected violations.

The code should also clearly state the consequences for violating the standards set forth in the code. Every employee should receive a copy of the code and should acknowledge not only receipt of the code but that he or she has read the code, understands it, and agrees to live by the ideals it sets forth.

Employee Training

Every employee must be trained so that he or she understands what is expected of the employee and what the employee can expect. Training should begin within the highest levels of the organization and encompass all employees. It should be developed so that its message is appropriate for the particular target audience and should be participative so that complete understanding is ensured. The persons used to deliver the training must thoroughly understand the self-governance program and must be skilled in presenting training programs. All training most clearly state that the self-governance program has received and will continue to receive the highest level of commitment from the company's top management.

New employees must be given training in the self-governance program as part of the company's orientation process. Like ongoing training, new-employee training should be tailored to the target audience, given the new employees' skills, positions, and responsibilities. Following the initial training, all employees should receive periodic training at appropriate intervals at least annually, to reinforce the program's objectives and to highlight any changes in the program.

Training should be geared to the specific target audience and should clearly inform employees of their obligations under the program.

Methods for reporting suspected violations and the investigative process should also be explained. Employees should feel they are part of an honest, hard-working team that endeavors to remain in compliance with the requirements of the company's self-governance program.

Reporting and Investigating

Self-governance implies not only that an organization will maintain written policies, systems, and controls for complying with pertinent requirements, but also that it will identify and act on instances of noncompliance. Careful thought must be given to this element of the program to avoid its perception as a negative, informant-type process. If that is not avoided, the entire self-governance program will have little impact on the activities of the organization. Employees will be overly cautious about reporting suspected violations and may even fear that notifying the company of a suspected violation could jeopardize their own job security. Employees will then assume the proper way to handle any suspected violation is to simply ignore it.

It is important that the company emphasize that all reports of suspected violations will be handled confidentially and that there will be no reprisals for a person filing a report in good faith. However, abuses of the system should not be tolerated and should entail disciplinary action.

Several alternative reporting mechanisms should be provided to employees. The initial decision as to how to report a particular suspected violation would then be left up to the employee. One reporting alternative would be to have an employee speak with his or her supervisor. This would allow the employee to discuss a suspected violation with an authority figure and would allow for open discussion of a problem. However, there may be cases where this alternative is not appropriate because the employee is not comfortable talking directly to his or her supervisor or, in some instances, because the supervisor may be the cause of the suspected violation. For example, a supervisor may insist that an employee alter his or her time sheet to charge time to a job other than the job actually worked. For situations such as this, an alternative reporting procedure must be provided, such as reporting to a department or division head or to an ombudsman. An ombudsman is a person who has demonstrated great personal integrity and is highly respected by the organization. An ombudsman may be a person within the company or an independent outside party. This person should be appointed with some degree of fanfare and publicity in order to draw attention to the position and to further show the company's commitment to the program. The ombudsman must have the full endorsement of top management and must be given the full authority to handle any matter brought to his or her attention.

The reporting system should facilitate reporting of suspected violations. Persons should be able to either call a hot-line number or file a written report. Again, all reports, no matter how made, should be kept in the utmost confidence. If a hot line is used, the tracing of calls coming in on the line should not be possible, and only the ombudsman should have access to the phone. Not even his or her secretary should have the authority to answer this line. It is not recommended that an answering device be installed on the hot-line phone as this may limit the degree of confidentiality afforded to employees.

Once a suspected violation is reported, the ombudsman must be empowered to investigate the allegation promptly. During the investigation stage it is imperative that employees be ensured that any report filed will be handled in confidence. The ombudsman must be given as much leeway as possible to conduct the investigation. However, care must be taken to ensure that the ombudsman does not violate any legal rights of employees during an investigation. Following an investigation, findings should be made as quickly as possible, and the employee reporting the violation should be made aware of the outcome. By doing this, the employee sees the outcome of reported problems and is assured that the system is working.

In short, the following process is usually followed for reports of suspected violations:

- The suspected violation is reported, and the case file is opened.
- The report recipient formally documents the report and logs it into a secure system.
- The suspected violation is reviewed to determine action needed—for example:
  —discussion with involved personnel
  —further review of conditions reported
  —formal investigation
  —no further action needed
- The action taken is documented in the case file.
- The conclusions reached are documented in the case file.
- Follow-up actions are determined and documented in the case file—for example:
  —revise or enhance written policies and procedures
  —revise or enhance systems and controls

—take appropriate disciplinary action

—provide input as appropriate to the training program

- The matter is reported in accordance with the self-governance program criteria, protecting the identity of the source.
- Feedback is provided to the reporting person, if possible.
- The case file is closed.

Disclosure

Investigations of suspected violations may indicate that a violation did, in fact, occur. In such cases it is essential that the investigation document the reason for, and the impact of, the violation. This is necessary not only to establish what internal action may be necessary, as previously discussed, but also to establish what external disclosures, if any, may be warranted. The following table presents examples of investigation findings and potential internal actions and disclosures that may be required:

Investigative Finding	Internal Actions	External Disclosures
• Technical violation of regulation; no adverse impact.	• Instruct employee. • Revise/clarify policy. • Enhance training.	• None.
• Billing error due to use of erroneous rates; isolated case and honest mistake; government was overcharged.	• Instruct employee.	• Administrative report to contracting officer. • Voluntary refund.
• Labor mischarging to avoid contractual ceiling; directed by program manager; government was overcharged.	• Take disciplinary action. • Strengthen controls.	• Voluntary disclosure to Inspector General. • Voluntary refund.

As indicated, if an external disclosure is deemed necessary, it could be either administrative or judicial in nature. If the activity involves illegal actions, a voluntary disclosure affords the company an opportunity to come forward and report on its investigation and actions taken. In many instances voluntary disclosure is looked on favorably by the government. This is not to say that no penalties will be paid; however, coming forward voluntarily may help reduce the severity of any penalties levied. For example, during the period January 1, 1989, through October 1, 1989, 73 companies voluntarily disclosed 164 instances of wrongdoing to the Department of Defense. In 155 of the 164 instances, no criminal sanctions were imposed on the contractors. Of the remaining nine instances, one was so severe that the government believed it could not avoid imposing criminal sanctions. In the remaining eight cases, the government was already aware of the activity at the time the disclosure was made. Thus, in over 94 percent of the cases disclosed, the companies were not assessed any criminal sanctions.

The subject of voluntary disclosure has been an emotional, and sometimes controversial, issue. However, companies that endorse self-governance believe that voluntary disclosure simply represents a responsible business practice that should be followed in the ordinary course of business.

Disciplinary Action

The self-governance program should include written statements of specific disciplinary actions that will be taken for violations of the code of conduct and for other instances of noncompliance. The disciplinary action should, of course, be appropriate to the severity of the violation. For example, a company may specify the following:

Nature of Violation	**Disciplinary Action**
• Unintentional violation; no adverse impact.	• None; employee counseled to ensure understanding.
• Noncompliance with minor (specify) monetary impact:	
— first offense	• Letter of reprimand.
— second offense	• One-day suspension with no pay.
— third offense	• Dismissal.
• Noncompliance with major (specify) monetary impact:	
— first offense	• One-day suspension with no pay.
— second offence	• Dismissal.
• Indicated intentional noncompliance with major monetary impact.	• Dismissal; legal action as appropriate.

These are simple examples of how a disciplinary action program might be structured. In reality, this is an extremely important and complex component of the self-governance program. All attributes relative to each form of violation and associated disciplinary actions must be clearly and completely spelled out and published. In setting disciplinary action, companies need to be as specific and realistic as possible. Published policy should specify the types of violations, such as using the company photocopier for personal business, accepting gratuities, giving gratuities to government personnel, giving kickbacks to vendors, mischarging for labor and falsifying documents or reports.

Once the disciplinary action program has been developed and published, the program must be enforced. This is another difficult aspect of self-governance, but one that must be followed precisely as set forth in the standards of conduct. Employee rights must be taken into account when taking disciplinary action. The denial of an employee's legal rights, even if inadvertent, can expose the company and its management to legal liability. For this reason the involvement of counsel is advisable.

Periodic Review

As with any program, a company's self-governance program should embody a system of review and oversight. The self-governance program needs to be reviewed regularly to ensure that it is working as intended and to identify needed updates and enhancements. For example, the standards of conduct should be reviewed at least annually. Changes in laws, regulations, policies, and practices could dictate changes in the standards of conduct.

The training program and its effectiveness also should be reviewed regularly to ensure that training continues to meet the needs of management and the work force. Over time, the demographics of the work force will change, and training that may have been appropriate for the work force of last year may no longer be appropriate for the current work force.

Files on suspected violations and their disposition should be reviewed periodically. This ensures that company policies are followed in terms of documenting the actions taken in reviewing and disposing of reports.

At the outset of a self-governance program it is not unusual for a company to experience an onslaught of reports of suspected misconduct. Often a large number of these early reports are frivolous or trivial and deal with activities that are beyond the bounds of company business. However, once the self-governance program becomes established, the incidence of such reports should dwindle. If they do continue, then it is possible that additional training and communications are needed. Conversely, if major problems are not uncovered by the self-governance program, then the company must reassess its approach in order to identify actions needed to make it effective.

If a company has an internal audit activity, the review of the self-governance program should be embodied in its annual audit plan. If there is no internal audit function, this review may be conducted by an ad hoc internal review team or by an outside organization engaged to perform the review. In any event, annual reviews of the self-governance program are essential to a successful, ongoing program.

Independent Audit

There is some criticism of the self-governance concept because it is internal to a company. For this reason companies often choose to have an independent third party review the program and report on the results of such audit, as is done in the DII program. Such an independent audit certainly lends credibility to the program and serves as a good check and balance on the effectiveness of the total program, including internal review. An independent auditor can be more objective than internal reviewers and can detect areas that may be overlooked or minimized by internal staff.

A self-governance program is structured around written policies, systems, and controls. A company's independent auditors are thoroughly familiar with a company's policies, systems, and controls and are trained in evaluating them. Further, professional literature calls for an independent CPA to assess the adequacy of internal controls as part of the annual financial audit. For this reason companies may look to their independent CPA to provide an annual independent audit of the self-governance program.

COMPANY COMMITMENT TO SELF-GOVERNANCE

As has been emphasized throughout this chapter, the cornerstone of any self-governance program is the commitment from the highest levels of the organization. A company cannot expect standards of conduct to be followed by employees without the strong example of top-level management. In addition, it is often the managers who must make an ethical choice between short-term profits and long-term public opinion, as in the Tylenol tampering incident. Such an instance sets corporate ethics and sets a positive public image.

Besides the responsibility to customers for product quality, companies have a responsibility to society to protect the environment. For years companies have operated just at the legal minima, dumping as much waste as was allowed into the waters and the air. As we become aware of the dangerous situation of the environment, companies are faced with another sort of ethical decision—disposing safely of waste byproducts, cleaning up after accidental spills, etc. Again, it is the managers who must effect the changes; yet it is the employees who must enforce them. The carelessness of one employee can damage the reputation of the entire company.

For a self-governance program to work, management and employees must work together. Standards of conduct should be clearly stated, written confirmation of understanding should be obtained from all employees, and these standards should be continually reasserted throughout an employee's tenure. Internal investigative procedures and disciplinary actions must be in place, and employees must be aware of them.

Regardless of the size of the company and the industry in which it is involved, a self-governance program is an important part of the corporate environment.

The self-governance model entails the seven key elements described in detail above. In order to implement a self-governance program, however, these elements must be thought of as one program. When a company decides to enact such a program, management should consider how each element will be addressed. Like any change, if it is announced prematurely, its chances for success are lessened.

When considering a self-governance program, a company should consider

- the organization's business mix—government versus commercial sales
- past experiences with self-governance activity
- the current status of any legal matter that involves fraud or other criminal allegation

In addition, the following specific areas may be affected by the implementation of a self-governance program, and any input to these areas should be understood:

- timekeeping practices
- accumulation of independent research and development
- bid and proposal costs
- expense reporting
- billing
- pricing/estimating
- gratuities

- marketing practices
- drug-free workplace
- audit procedures

When a company's current corporate culture does not have a strong self-governance element, managers must begin to reevaluate the company's method of doing business. If they are to be successful in the future, a self-governance program should be implemented now.

7

Corporate Counsel's Role in Interactive Compliance

Joseph E. Murphy

According to some people, corporate lawbreaking appears to be the norm in an anything-goes business world. Insider trading, government contract fraud, bid rigging, and uncontrolled hazardous waste dumping are all part of the "popular" image of business. And what of the lawyers who deal with the corporate behemoths? They are neatly divided into the white hats and the black hats. The white hats are worn by the embattled plaintiffs' lawyers who bring villainous corporate scoundrels to their knees and by the U.S. attorneys who replace pinstripes with prison stripes. The villains in black represent the defendants' bar and are known as unctuous mouthpieces who help the rich wrongdoers escape the law.

In this setting what is the role of the corporate counsel who is the legal representative of the corporation? Is it his or her responsibility to prevent the company from breaking the law? Are corporate counsel the designated conscience of business? For some corporate counsel the answer is that compliance is management's responsibility. They see their role as advisor, or as pit bull—but not as watchdog. Some managers see the law as the business of the lawyers. They

This chapter is based on material prepared for *The Pennsylvania Lawyer, The Lawyer's Brief,* and *The ACCA Docket*. The opinions expressed are those of the author and not necessarily those of any institution with which he is associated.

believe that counsel should take care of the "legal stuff," while they run the business.

WHAT IS CORPORATE COUNSEL'S ROLE IN COMPLIANCE?

Neither of these descriptions is correct, but they both contain a certain amount of wisdom. The best corporate legal advice includes all the steps necessary to anticipate and avoid risks; it also includes a forecast of the long-term legal consequences of corporate actions. If the corporate client fails to consider the legal environment, in the long run it will face the painful consequences of punitive legislation, business taxes, abusive consent decrees, disruptive litigation, and the spread of an unsympathetic legal system. In the simplest terms, the difference between doing what is "legal" and doing what is "ethical" may be just the length of one legislative session. It may not take Congress or a state legislature very long to get even with companies that try to live on loopholes.

Even beyond the dollars-and-cents duty to the client, corporate counsel, as members of the legal profession, are subject to other obligations. The general apathy that has created a void where effective compliance programs should be is not in the interest of our children, our neighborhoods, or our wallets: All are the victims of ethical sloth in business. If corporate counsel do not wish to help guide business behavior, someone else is likely to fill the void. Corporate counsel who ignore these professional responsibilities may find themselves wearing the black hat due to their inaction.

Accepting that corporate counsel have a duty to do more than just blindly follow the orders of company management, how is that duty defined? Given that many management officials are not motivated even to discuss a compliance program until a grand jury subpoena arrives, it is therefore corporate counsel's role to help management implement compliance programs, acting as a catalyst, a guide, and a tool.

Sadly, corporate counsel practicing preventive law and fulfilling their professional responsibility through compliance initiatives bear the additional responsibility of explaining to the corporate client the dangers of a compliance program that is too good. An ambitious compliance program, including audits and evaluations of employees' legal performance, can be a very risky business for the company. Government prosecutors, plaintiffs' lawyers, and skeptical judges will all look to the materials produced in such campaigns as necessary for use in lawsuits attacking the corporation's failures in the realm of compliance, while at the same time debunking corporate protests as mere obstructions to the search for "everyman's evidence." In one case, a plaintiff actually incorporated a copy of a company's business conduct guidelines into its complaint.

WHAT IS NEEDED FOR A COMPLIANCE PROGRAM?

If counsel, or any other compliance-oriented corporate groups, are inclined to push for effective compliance programs, what must they do? Certainly there are many programs in many companies, and thrifty counsel might be tempted to save time and effort by just picking up what has been done somewhere else and bringing it home. Is there really a need for anything more than this?

With all of the attention that has been given to at least some areas of corporate compliance, a debilitating narrowness of focus has remained in this work. Nor can those who work in compliance point proudly to outstanding results. One need only look at each morning's *Wall Street Journal* headlines on the latest business indictments to reach this conclusion.

To gather some insight on why this might be, we can look at a hypothetical situation involving an imaginary corporation, Synergy Communications. Synergy's sales are off; management has decided to recast its sales program and calls in two experts—a compliance expert and a sales manager. Applying what they have learned from their own activities, what type of program would each set up?

One suspects that the compliance expert would do this: He would start with a 25-page booklet written by an accountant— or, more likely, five different accountants—explaining the importance of selling. He would have a financial analyst write a statement for the company's chief executive officer to sign, announcing the company's commitment to selling. Once a year he would bring in another high-priced financial analyst to give a lecture on the importance of selling and to warn of dire consequences if sales fall flat. The compliance expert's bottom line message would be "Bad things will happen if you don't sell." This program would offer no rewards, no bonuses, no controls, and no excitement. In fact, the compliance expert has no real knowledge of what works, but he does know that he has always used these methods before.

What would the second expert, the sales manager, do when facing the fact that her career depends on increasing sales? She would tie the salespeople's pay to their performance and develop measurement systems to see who is selling and who is not. She would bring the CEO in when necessary to meet with major customers, and the CEO would be there to commend the top salespeople. She would survey customers for feedback so the company would know why customers refused its sales approach and what changes need to be made. Training would be critical. Every salesperson would have drilled into him or her that the customer is king. Each would also have hands-on training on the products and would practice simulated sales presentations.

The sales manager would create excitement for the sales force. Every week and every month she would celebrate the top salesperson—the company's hero. Each time a major product was sold, bells would go off in the local sales office. Her bottom-line message to the sales force would be "Join the team and sell, and you'll get money and praise."

Choosing between these two approaches, which one is likely to be more effective in motivating people? Yet consider which one is usually selected to deal with corporate conduct in compliance and business ethics. Fundamentally, ethics and compliance are matters of corporate management. If we are going to reach business conduct, we must use the same tools that corporate managers use to get results.

If we follow this concept, three basic rules are fundamental to any compliance program:

1. Actively involve senior management.
2. Use results-oriented education and awareness programs.
3. Make compliance a part of management's system of incentives and controls.

The following tips incorporate these fundamentals and are intended to provide the starting point for a compliance program. Not all this advice will apply to all situations, nor is every consideration listed. Corporate counsel should use these guidelines as a starting point to design a program that will fit their company's unique needs. Counsel may also wish to refer to Michael Goldblatt's *Preventive Law in Corporate Practice* (1989) for a comprehensive overview of the elements to include in a compliance program.

1. *Have senior management participate in a compliance workshop, including a discussion with a convicted white collar felon or other "reformed sinner."* Do not underestimate the value of presenting a brief, hard-hitting meeting for senior managers with a speaker who has "been there" and knows what it is like to violate the rules and pay for it; this kind of presentation has a lasting impact on participants. If possible, get the fullest impact by presenting the program away from the office, telephone messages, and anyone else who might

interrupt. For more information on the use of convicted felons in compliance programs, see Jeffrey M. Kaplan's chapter herein on "Scared Straight" programs for the business community and his "Making the Most of Sentencing" (1988).

2. *Include legal compliance in the annual evaluation of senior managers.* If managers' performance levels are measured on the basis of an issue, they will pay more attention to that issue. Production and profit, which are invariably subject to constant measuring, are important, but so is playing by the rules. Rejecting this theory out of hand as impractical or too difficult to implement is tempting because measuring compliance is like measuring any other negative: How do you measure what was prevented?

Creating such an incentive system will require substantial focus and thought. Bear in mind, however, that the development of a system to measure profits and production also forces a company to analyze subjective elements in allocating fault and rewards. While not every element of compliance can be quantified, some—for instance, pollution levels and worker safety—clearly are easily quantified. Others—such as commitment to fair competition principles—will require more subjective analysis and greater creativity. Surveys of a manager's subordinates to test their training in and understanding of the relevant compliance rules may be a starting point.

Take care in this sort of evaluation that the results cannot be used to hurt the company in pending or subsequent litigation. The assessment standards should be those of the company's policies, which should cut even wider than the law. (See item 10 below.) Also, counsel who are familiar with the attorney-client and self-evaluative privileges should provide guidance in the creation of any such program. Use the same caution with the compliance audits discussed in item 13.

3. *Have regular reports on compliance efforts to the board of directors.* What is really important to your company? What answer would you find from a review of your board's minutes? As suggested by the Treadway Commission (*Report of the National Commission on Fraudulent Financial Reporting* 1987, 35), at least an audit committee of the board or senior management should be aware of what is being done to monitor compliance with the company's code of conduct. Such a practice also serves the indispensable purpose of assuring that internal compliance groups have a source of power other than the line managers they are required to monitor.

4. *Use compliance seminars, augmented by publications and videotapes showing the personal impact of noncompliance.* In the antitrust area it has been suggested on several occasions that failure to use the commercially produced videotape *The Price* in compliance seminars is almost tantamount to malpractice. The most effective

presentations create audience identification with the message and command the viewers' attention. While videos are helpful in this regard, they are weak in promoting analysis and problem-solving techniques. Therefore, multimedia presentations should be used to completely cover the general issues and your company's and industry's particulars. See item 6 below for guidance on how to interact with the audience and encourage audience participation.

Many counsel have found that creating their own video can help to solve the apathy problem and surely will attract the attention and focus of the target audience. Some videomaking tips: Be humble and hire professionals to do the job—you may be a great lawyer, but are probably inexperienced as a director. Likewise, remember that good brief writers may not be good dialogue writers, and good employees may be wooden as actors. Build conflicts into the story—two lawyers agreeing with each other on television is always boring.

5. *Require seminar attendance for bonus eligibility.* This step serves two important purposes: It gets people to show up, and it ties compliance into the company's value system (i.e., the paycheck). Do not allow exceptions; remember that the people with the least time for attending seminars are the people you need to target most.

6. *Have the seminar presenter interact with the attendees.* If attendees do not talk, they do not learn; this is especially true in matters of compliance. Unless you are planning to give a written examination that will be graded afterward, forget lectures, and keep groups small in order to promote interaction among and contributions from every member of the group. A good way to encourage this conversation is to ask questions of each participant (without intimidating them) or to let attendees role-play lawyers giving you advice or jurors or prosecutors examining the company's products or records.

7. *Field-test all compliance material with line managers.* If compliance materials will not work for those responsible for their implementation, solicit input of the dissatisfied, and change the approach. Compliance lawyers have a case to make, and the jury is made up of line managers. Just because the lawyers in your office like your compliance design does not mean that the program will work for the line managers. While you cannot compromise your legal message, you must negotiate the medium with those responsible for its success or failure, incorporate their input, and respond to their reactions.

8. *Offer to preview draft compliance materials with the appropriate government enforcement agency.* This step is one of the key points in moving toward an interactive compliance program. If government is serious about its policies, it should help and encourage counsel working to increase compliance. This is not to suggest that you should delude yourself about the current agency approach. If you are very

fortunate, agency officials may review the material and tell you they agree with you. They may even offer substantive comments and advise you of other available resources. This kind of "clearance" can be invaluable evidence of your compliance efforts and your program's sufficiency if later problems arise or if a plaintiff attempts to use the program against you. Even if the government refuses to review the material, the offer acts as evidence of your good faith.

9. *Measure the seminar's impact and staying power. Expand what does work and drop what does not.* I once had a manager ask me, in response to my request that his people attend a compliance seminar, whether I could show any benefit from attendance at the seminar. At the time I thought this was a rather irreverent bit of sarcasm, but on reflection I find it touches one of the major weaknesses of the available approaches to compliance. Managers *should* ask what works, and counsel should be able to provide an answer. Test your audiences six months after a presentation (and again after a year) to see what they remember, what made an impression, and what flopped; fix your presentations accordingly. Find out if employees are reading the literature you distribute. Do they remember the speakers or actors in a video, but forget the message? Use this information in creating programs that even sarcastic managers will agree benefit the corporation.

10. *Provide written compliance guidelines in conversational style, explaining the company's policies. Do not restate the law; do not use language that sounds like the U.S. Code.* Today, practically every major company has written business conduct guidelines, usually requiring sign-off by employees. Yet even such a fundamental step is not without risk. If the guidelines purport to state the law, there is a real possibility that they will be used against the company in litigation to establish a violation of the law by showing a violation of the guidelines. The accepted wisdom therefore is that the guidelines should state policy, not law, and should recite that the company's policy sweeps beyond the requirements of the law.

Guidelines should not be restatements of the U.S. Code. If you must cover every "whereas," "wherefore," and possible loophole, put all that detail in a three-ring binder and distribute one copy to each work location. Annotate it on a regular basis, and keep it available for your litigation lawyers to use in showing that employees were on notice about all the fine points. But do not assume that many employees will ever look at it.

To be effective, guidelines must be readable and user friendly. Use illustrations, bullet points, and sidebars. Refer to the three-ring binder for the fine print and for the loopholes and details. Above all, remember that guidelines alone will not do anything to change the compliance record of a company; they are only a tool to be used intelligently by management. See Mathews' *Strategic Intervention in Organizations* (1988), reporting that companies with conduct books have no better compliance records than those without them.

11. *Require acquisition and new business plans to include compliance programs.* Compliance work should be part of the basic activities of a company. When managers think about the future of the business, they should be encouraged also to focus on the necessary compliance objectives. One way to encourage this commitment is to include compliance programs and the legal challenges the company will face as a part of any plans designed to assess future acquisitions and profit and production projections.

12. *Establish a corporate ombudsman with unquestioned integrity, easy accessibility for complaints, organizational independence, full senior management and legal department support, and access to the board of directors.* The ombudsman is one of the best potential compliance tools available; yet it is one of the least recognized by corporate counsel. An effective ombudsman can serve to vent problems internally, before they explode externally. The ombudsman serves as an outlet for customers, competitors, suppliers, and employees, encouraging communication with the corporation before communication with the press or a lawyer.

In every compliance area—EEO, antitrust, the environment, and so on—someone in the company knows "what is going on." These potential whistleblowers—whether secretaries, auditors, retirees, mail clerks, or disgruntled officers—can become a prime resource for uncovering incipient problems before they reach the violation stage. But if employees are not offered a safe harbor within the company—someone they can trust to listen and take effective action when warranted—this valuable opportunity will be lost. The ombudsman is successful in this endeavor where others are not because the ombudsman can keep reports confidential and act as protector for the employee who wants to present a concern, but is afraid of retaliation.

In order for the ombudsman to work as a lightning rod for problems, the corporation must dedicate the resources necessary to ensure his or her effectiveness. The ombudsman must have direct access to the real power in the organization. He or she must not report to a sales or line organization, but to a vice-president or higher officer. That person should also have priority access to the company's best compliance lawyer. If there is a compliance committee, the ombudsman should be in constant communication with and contribute substantively to that group. Ultimately, the ombudsman should be vested with the power to report directly to the board any refusals by management to take corrective action where known compliance violations exist.

Although the ombudsman is a strong voice for compliance efforts, he or she may present a significant risk to the corporation, given the current litigation environment. The ombudsman should be protected by a strong self-evaluative privilege to immunize his or her work from discovery. Until such a shield is available, however, the ombudsman must work with counsel to minimize these risks by keeping sparse notes and carefully worded written reports.*

13. *Audit compliance, but always use counsel for such projects, and write only what you would not hesitate to show to a jury.* Internal reviews are essential and serve many useful functions for counsel and corporation. However, the internal review process involves a great deal of peril if done without forethought. Reviews should be performed only by experienced counsel, taking all necessary steps to preserve privilege claims. Under the right circumstances there are three forms of protection: the attorney-client privilege, the work-product doctrine (technically not a privilege), and the self-evaluative privilege. Before conducting your first audit, invest some time in researching this subject. As a starting point, both the American Corporate Counsel Association and the National Center for Preventive Law at the University of Denver College of Law may be able to provide some informational materials. The research list should also include a recent book by the dean of preventive law, Louis Brown, and his coauthor, Anne Kandel, entitled *The Legal Audit: Corporate Internal Investigation* (1990).

In your internal review, use care in generating written reports, include the resolution of any flaws you find, and write a piece you would be proud to read to a jury. Never assume any privilege will prevail. Save the attention-getting language for your oral presentations (and remind the audience, "no notes, please"). And, most importantly, be sure management is prepared to act immediately on your findings, or you may have given ammunition to the plaintiff who discovers your unheeded recommendations.

14. *Manage compliance by drawing on the same incentives, rewards, and control techniques used to manage sales and production.* One of the best sources for compliance ideas is management literature. Observe how such literature sets up the motivation to meet sales objectives. What rewards will you offer in your compliance programs for those who project and maintain positive role models? What

*Information on establishing a corporate ombudsman is available from the Corporate Ombudsman Association, 14 Wynkoop Court, Bethesda, MD 20817.

deterrents will aberrant behavior generate? We have no right to expect that compliance programs will come easily to us; after all, no other management program does. If a half-hour video every six months will not make a company profitable, why would we assume it will make the company ethical?

An example reported in the *Washington Post* (Webb, 1990) shows in basic terms the importance of using rewards to deal with corporate conduct and of recognizing it is incentives that drive people to perform, and not just a desire to avoid harm. A major Washington, D.C., bakery had a substantial problem with worker injury and lost employee time. As a result, the bakery instituted a very simple program of incentives. When a work group passed 110 days without a lost workday, each member received $20. If it went another 120 days, each member received $30, and after a year, $50.

The bakery's reward program has been dramatically successful, with an 82 percent decline in lost workdays. The article even quoted an employee as saying, "If I've got to prop him up with a broomstick, he's coming to work." Business incentives are an effective tool, providing the maximum impact when they cause work groups to reinforce the message.

15. *At all stages, believe in the values behind the program, apply good management techniques, and use experienced counsel.* If the program you design is just for the record, you may as well not bother. This cynicism may actually generate a noncompliance environment. Woe to the counsel who underestimates the ability of the company's informal intelligence network to discern and broadcast a lax compliance attitude; if counsel and senior executives do not buy into the program, you can be sure the employees will react accordingly. Doubters should consider the experience of General Electric's antitrust compliance program of the 1950s; the violations resulting from that program's failures resulted in years of civil and criminal prosecutions.

Compliance is a joint responsibility of management and counsel; an effective program combines the best resources of both groups and a commitment to follow through. Although litigation pitfalls abound, understanding how to motivate, educate, and simplify the law for the company's managers will enable them to implement an effective and defensible compliance program in day-to-day business activities. If counsel do not succeed in designing programs that make compliance workable, and thereby do not convince managers to assume their share of the responsibility for their bad acts or inaction, it is only to be expected that government agencies or the courts will take over the responsibility for regulating corporations. History has demonstrated that such regulation will entail programs far more onerous in their intrusions and costs (yet ultimately less effective) than would a program of self-maintenance.

COUNSEL'S ROLE IN MOVING TO AN INTERACTIVE ENVIRONMENT

Corporate counsel who lead their companies to implement effective compliance programs can rightly take great pride in that accomplishment—but it is not enough. It was only partly in jest that the maxim "No good deed goes unpunished" was created, and counsel must face the unfortunate disincentives, created mostly by the legal system, that work against the development of effective compliance programs. Both the litigation risks created by such programs and the absence of tangible benefits to high-complying companies are factors that counsel, working with other like-minded groups, should address. Counsel should take the lead in changing government's approach and moving toward an interactive relationship.

Counsel's counterparts in government must be given a better understanding of how corporations are managed and the value of positive incentives in this process. It should not be so difficult to understand that fear alone is not the prime, or even the most effective, motivator of conduct. Those who believe in compliance efforts need to drive home to government the importance of government's putting something on the table—a reward for positive behavior. This, in turn, gives the compliance-oriented groups like company counsel something they can offer their fellow managers as an inducement. It gives these compliance groups a measurable objective to work for: obtaining the government's incentives for their company.

The importance of compliance incentives also touches on a fact of corporate life that those outside simply overlook. There is much that corporate counsel and other compliance-oriented groups can and should do in voluntary programs. But corporate lawyers, like all corporate managers, have numerous demands competing for their time. Will a company devote a lawyer's time to product safety review committees when that same lawyer is responsible for negotiating a major sales contract with a customer? When budgets must be cut to satisfy the new chief financial officer, what will compliance counsel offer to defend compliance program expenditures? Priorities within companies are set by revenue impacts. Lucrative contracts and angry litigants are immediate needs; it will often appear that long-term avoidance of legal risks can be deferred. The opportunity for tangible rewards can go far to readjust management's priorities regarding compliance.

This proposition is a simple one, but one that is rarely discussed with government. It is all well and good for a compliance lawyer to say to a client, "If you are bad and you get caught, you will get punished." The problem is that the good clients do not believe they are doing something "bad," and the bad clients do not think they will get caught. It is far more effective if counsel can say, "Yes, if you do something wrong, you will get caught and punished. But if you do what I suggest, you will have an advantage over your competitors, and my proposed compliance program will bring benefits four times greater than the cost of this program." This is a *management* approach to compliance, but it takes a commitment from government.

One recent example makes this point. The Baldrige Quality Awards are high-visibility honors offered to corporate leaders in quality. These have had dramatic effects, considering that their sole payoff is publicity. Corporations are scrambling for this award. One of the last winners, Xerox, took out a full-page ad in the *Wall Street Journal* trumpeting the fact that it had won this certification. Publicity, and other rewards available to government, could have the same effect in inducing competition for developing effective compliance programs.

Counsel should also confront the direct threats to compliance activities created by the litigation system. Rather than passively accepting the anomaly that positive compliance efforts may be exploited to harm a company, counsel should champion efforts to change the law. They should focus most specifically on efforts to strengthen and legislate a self-evaluative privilege.

In a substantial number of cases courts have accepted a qualified protection for corporate self-evaluative reviews. The protection offered is too weak and too unpredictable to serve its purpose, however. What is needed is a substantial immunity that recognizes that internal reviews have been critically weakened by the constant exposure to risk in litigation and that they will become fully effective only when they are both encouraged and protected by government. Endorsement of a self-evaluative privilege would be an important step in government's recognizing the need to help counsel in convincing clients to audit compliance.

Corporate counsel can best follow the agenda set forth here—both in developing internal programs and in changing the external environment—by working with the organized bar and other groups that share this direction. It is in counsel's interest to seek greater recognition of the importance of compliance work and to seek more attention for the development and testing of various techniques. In this effort, counsel should also call on the law schools to participate actively. This, too, would work to create a basis for interaction between academia and the corporate bar.

Corporate counsel can join with their counterparts at other corporations to organize developmental activities. These would include workshops and institutes on developing compliance techniques. Ultimately, law schools would be expected to recognize compliance and similar preventive law elements in their curricula, displacing current litigation-heavy approaches.

Counsel's work in the bar should invite interaction with their regulatory, enforcement, and legislative counterparts in government. Participation in this process will emphasize the fundamentally common purpose of all participants in managing corporations for compliance, without exclusive reliance on restrictive legislation and penalties. Through these steps, counsel can maximize legal protection for their clients, while taking a substantial stride toward the type of interactive environment that will boost corporate lawfulness at reduced cost to business and society.

8

Corporate Lawbreakers as Sources of Interactive Training

Jeffrey M. Kaplan

Every company faces its own particular compliance problems, but all face the same overriding challenge: to make law and ethics come alive in the work place.

Consider the following hypothetical situation (which could easily be adapted to virtually any business setting). A sales executive instructs a subordinate to prepare and sign what is obviously a complementary bid. There is initial resistance, but the executive makes it unmistakably clear that this is an order—not a request—and that the subordinate will deeply regret any refusal to follow orders. The executive says that he wants the bid completed immediately—and that he won't leave the subordinate's office until he receives it.

The next ten seconds may be critical in the life of both the subordinate and the company. Once he has gone along even with one criminal act, it may be very difficult for the subordinate to resume his prior state of happy lawfulness. The executive will always have additional leverage to command obedience in the criminal enterprise, and, in any event, the subordinate will probably begin to rationalize his participation.

If the scheme is uncovered, the wrong choice made during these ten seconds could be nothing short of ruinous. For the individual there is a high likelihood of prison, particularly under the federal sentencing guidelines; the loss of employment and future employability; and, often, psychological devastation to family members, which the offender regrets most of all.

For the company there may be massive criminal penalties, treble damages civil exposure, substantial attorneys' fees, possible debarment in the case of government contractors, and the potentially fatal loss of customer confidence and employee morale.

How, then, do we reach this employee so that he does the right thing during the most important and stressful ten seconds of his life?

SCARED STRAIGHT

Perhaps the stern words of warning against bid rigging in the company's policy booklet will come to mind at the critical moment. The chances are, however, that those words have long since gone to the back of the brain, to be warehoused with scores of other commandments and admonitions. Indeed, one major survey of corporate codes of ethics concluded that "there is little relationship between codes of conduct and corporate violations, contrary to the expectation that the codes serve as an effective form of self-regulation" (Mathews 1988, 76).

To be effective, the warning must be memorable enough to counteract the terrifying immediacy of the executive, with his undoubted power over the subordinate's economic well-being. This is a tall order indeed. What the subordinate—and the company—really need is a "little angel" who will pop up on the subordinate's shoulder (to borrow an image from cartoons) and whisper words of deterrence into his ear.

This is the idea behind the Scared Straight program being developed for future members of the business community by the Business Ethics Study Team, Inc. (BEST)—a New York–based nonprofit group affiliated with the Stern School of Business, New York University. BEST's program seeks out convicted white collar offenders to speak about their experiences in business school classrooms and to teach—in a personal, memorable way—the lesson that business crime does not pay.

White collar offenders have, of course, given lectures before. But these have tended to be well-known figures in widely publicized scandals, and their presentations may inadvertently convey the impression that only the big players—typically greedy, malevolent, or willful —are prosecuted. They may provide a false sense of comfort—"I could never do what *that* person did—and will ill prepare the listener for those critical ten seconds when trouble comes looking for him or her.

BEST's program therefore seeks out not the white collar masterminds, but their helpers—men and women caught up in (and ruined by) a crime of someone else's making. Typical is one man who, after graduating from a leading MBA program, went to work for a family business selling specialty pipe (used, for example, in nuclear plants and fossil fuel refineries). He found that virtually everyone in this entire industry had, for as long as could be remembered, routinely submitted inflated invoices on cost-plus jobs. He personally did not want to be involved in this practice, but felt he had no practical choice. Besides, he believed, since this was a crime of someone else's design and since *he* never profited personally from it, there was no question of his ever being prosecuted.

Time and changing prosecutorial priorities proved him wrong. Two years after coming out of prison, he has yet to find meaningful employment. To hear him speak is to learn that even minimum security jails are lousy places to be, that the stigma of a felony conviction follows one forever, and that worse than either of these is having to explain to one's children what has happened and hear them cry themselves to sleep.

Can individuals such as the pipe salesman become the angels who will pop up on employees' shoulders to provide lifesaving counsel when the critical time comes? The student reactions to BEST's experiment are thus far very encouraging:

- One student said that the presentation "was the single most thought provoking session of any in my business school career. I thought about his situation for days, and I still do."
- Another student observed that, like the offender, he, too, was "married with three kids," and this student found particularly haunting "the thought of doing what [the offender] had to do—going home to explain that I've been indicted. . . ."
- Still another student commented that "The best professor could not teach what [the offender] talked about. I could never risk the shame of jail. I think I'd rather die."

The image of a person devastated by his own weakness or blindness can indeed be a powerful form of deterrence, in precisely the same way that meeting a heart attack victim is a more powerful form of warning than is reading a newspaper article about the dangers of cholesterol. Deterrence with a human face can also make a company's code of ethics come alive and *stay* alive and be there when it is needed. Thus, BEST hopes to provide speakers to businesses as well as business schools. For a company and its employees, learning from someone else's mistakes may be the most effective and safest method of instruction.

AN INTERACTIVE CORPORATE COMPLIANCE EXPERIMENT

In *Interactive Corporate Compliance: An Alternative to Regulatory Compulsion* (1988), Jay A. Sigler and Joseph E. Murphy offer a vision of and a program for greater government-business cooperation in preventing corporate lawbreaking. This entails, in part, two major types of cooperation: (1) actual government involvement in designing and implementing compliance programs and (2) government incentives for extra compliance efforts.

The Scared Straight program offers a promising ground for testing both of these aspects of interactive corporate compliance. First, the program requires—or at least will greatly benefit from—government involvement in selecting offenders who are appropriate for the presentations (i.e., remorseful, articulate men and women who were criminal helpers and not originators). Not only are prosecutors best situated to do this, but also their involvement will undoubtedly make participation in the program more comfortable for some host institutions. The author has recently spoken with several prosecutors who have voiced a willingness—at least on an informal level—to help BEST seek out such offenders.

Additionally, the program may require government to confer a benefit for extra compliance efforts, albeit in a somewhat different sense than is envisioned by Sigler and Murphy. That is, it may be helpful for prosecutors to promise a reward to appropriate offenders to encourage their participation in the program. Specifically, prosecutors might choose to help offenders seek *some* prison sentence reduction; however, a complete reduction would reduce the efficacy of the offenders' presentations.

As a threshold matter, this latter type of cooperation may prove politically troublesome for some prosecutors, but ultimately it should not be an obstacle, as the program does serve many of the same interests as traditional forms of punishment. It has significant rehabilitative potential. Offenders are given a chance to find meaning and value in what is otherwise a totally negative—indeed nightmarish—experience. Instead of being merely the passive subjects of deterrence, they become bearers of an important message. The opportunity to be someone's guardian angel—to prevent future crimes and future misery—has at least as much rehabilitative potential as anything offered by the criminal justice system.

Second, the program is also as socially valuable as more traditional forms of cooperation with prosecutors, which routinely are rewarded in the sentencing process. While one cannot quantify this (or, for that matter, any other form of deterrence), even if only one offender reaches one student, his or her message may one day prevent tremendous harm to many.

Finally, the program touches another aspect of the Sigler-Murphy proposal: making compliance "a field of study" unto itself. That is, BEST plans to make the selected offenders (and materials related to their cases) available to research scholars. Thus, the program should give rise to an unprecedented opportunity for studying the failure of existing corporate compliance efforts (and law enforcement strategies) and for designing alternative approaches.

9

Competition and Climate in Law Schools

Thomas L. Shaffer

In their 1988 book, *Interactive Corporate Compliance,* Jay A. Sigler and Joseph E. Murphy noted that American legal education contributes to the use of litigation and confrontation in dispute resolution. Lawyers are not usually trained in negotiating, counseling, or reducing adversary tensions. Our research shows that a student's life in law school is one of endless competition. Progress in law school depends on competition far more than does progress in the practice of law.

THE COMPETITIVE MODEL OF EDUCATION

Competition in law school for the law review staff, for the moot court teams, for clinical programs, and for grades and status is intense. There is a relentless sorting out of people into first, second, and third; into top student, next student, and others. This kind of regimented rivalry hardly encourages a spirit of cooperation. The competitive climate of law schools must be changed if greater cooperation is to be brought into the public and the private sectors.

This law school process operates in and out of the classroom, through law professor models, from unarticulated attitudes among students, and from a general ambience in the place that traces even to members of the community who are no longer present at the school. Even climate is an educational force.

Law schools resemble one another in climate more than most law schools resemble other educational communities. Almost any law student would recognize the sights, the smells, and the mood of almost any law school. Nonetheless, variety among law schools is said to be wider and deeper in relation to dimensions of climate than it is in relation to course content, background of students, faculty teaching methods, or the contents of the law library. Law professors who recruit new law students at undergraduate colleges tend to speak cautiously when they "sell" their faculties or their books, but they speak with more conviction when they talk of the "character" of their schools. Character may, in a recruiting speech, mean prestige, pride, warmth, or local influence. In more negative discourse, character may mean hostility, coldness, destructive competition, or the tense emotional ambience created by interpersonal rivalry. To the extent that goals and purposes are seriously implicit in a law school, they can probably be traced to a primary commitment to professional training, which virtually all schools share, and to a diverse aggregation of influences that vary somewhat from school to school, most of which comprise climate.

It is climate more than structure or curriculum that earns for the Harvard Law School its reputation of commitment to excellence. It is the almost universal (if perhaps unexamined) view of lawyers that, whatever legal education does, Harvard does it best. Climate lends Denver and Yale a reputation for concern with social science and gives Virginia, Duke, Michigan, and Boalt (California-Berkeley) strong regional identification. Climate even more clearly is the source in smaller schools (Notre Dame, Washington and Lee, and Valparaiso) of a certain character of warmth and community closeness.

The point can be illustrated by the means a proponent of utopian education might use if he or she set out to create a humanistic law school, meaning one that emphasizes the needs of human beings. That task may be undertaken by adding "humane" subjects to the curriculum; employing broadly trained, cross-disciplinary law professors; defining course content with value objectives in mind; selecting students on the basis of criteria relating to concern and promise for human service; or selecting teachers and teaching methods that are particularly sensitive to the needs and dispositions of the students.

Yale is widely regarded as having experimented broadly with the addition of behaviorally oriented subjects to its curriculum; Denver has attempted, more than most schools, to employ law professors who are not (or not merely) lawyers, but also teachers in a value-oriented curriculum. Several schools have experimented with goal-centered admissions.

None of these experiments has been conspicuously successful, all of them require a significant political effort among law faculties and other boards of control, and all express in an institutional way a yearning for human service. For the most part, students find that law school frustrates their humanistic instincts.

Reformers of structure may overlook the possibility that change is frustrated by the law school climate. In other words, curriculum reform and value-centered admissions will not change the law school climate because climate is broader than the classroom and because it is clear that law students admitted in the traditional way already have more humanism than legal education can put to use. Curriculum reform should consider that law students are competitive people; they tend to struggle with and fuss at one another as juncos do on a snowy morning when all the bird seed is in one spot. Law professors are single-minded about the force of persuasion as a teaching technique and about the virtues of control. Lawyers who hire law students yearn for the signs and scars of academic battle; they tend to overvalue such things as class rank and essays published in the law review. These are human forces that tend to create a combative climate that course content and even admissions are not able to reform. They are aggravated by the fact that law grades are only given once or twice a year—and by the fact that rank of some sort is the only gold star in law school. Students who are not likely to thrive on three years of ambiguous combat, even if they come to law school disposed to competition, cope with the combative climate by emotional withdrawal or by what Erving Goffman (1959, 38–45) calls *secondary adjustment.*

Students who withdraw will not do without human relationships; they will find them outside of law school—among family, friends, church, undergraduate classmates, or even barbershop quartets. The effect of this defensive device on the students themselves is a sense of alienation from their professional associates (fellow students), which they may or may not overcome later when they find that fellow lawyers are (contrary to the myth) not as combative as law students are. The effect of student withdrawal on the law school is the enforcement of an impersonal climate: Professors lecture, then disappear; students seem not to know one another; few use names, and then rarely first names. The place tends to be more or less like an airline terminal.

Secondary adjustment may tend to cause rebellion of one sort or another. Withdrawal and secondary adjustment are alike in that they are both alternatives to an advertent and educationally functional learning climate. They are psychologically immediate ways for students to survive and to protect their own delicate tenderness in an otherwise combative, cold human community. It is possible to include climate within the regimen for humanistic legal education; it may, in fact, be fatal to humanistic objectives not to plan for climate when one plans for courses, professors, and the selection of students.

Law students' statements indicate that they are in significant part attracted to the legal profession because they are concerned with justice and have an interest in professional interpersonal relationships. Data that I gathered with Robert S. Redmount and that we discussed in our 1977 book, *Lawyers, Law Students, and People,* indicate that these dispositions are frustrated (but not destroyed) by law school and that students find little reinforcement or deepening of them as they study law. Personal remarks from students add to these data an impression that the effects of law school on personal concern with justice and on personal concern with people are aspects of *climate.*

We detected a number of significant elements in these remarks: Law students are, as a rule, competitive and aggressive; they are given to interpersonal styles that emphasize explanation (in words) and order. Their taste for competition, aggression, and verbalization helps explain their choice of the legal profession. In one way or another, our respondents confirm all of this. But our students also said that they expected to channel their competitiveness, aggression, and verbal order into skills and habits that would serve justice and foster interpersonal relationships. They said that their concern with justice was frustrated by law school and that their desire for interpersonal relationships was not converted into useful skills.

A few students, who give deliberate attention to their dispositions to be interpersonally helpful, believe that humanistic lawyering qualities can be learned (or at least reinforced) in legal education. And almost all law students believe law school should provide training in these skills. Each of these attitudes merits somewhat more extended consideration.

STUDENT ATTITUDES TOWARD LAW SCHOOL

1. *Law students are competitive, but they expect legal education to channel their competitiveness into skills that serve the ends of justice and interpersonal helpfulness.* Law students are aggressive people,

and they expect law school to make something useful out of their relish for combat. But they also expect their lives as lawyers to be open to more rewarding human experiences. As one student said:

> I would never disagree with the proposition that the lawyer must be fully committed to her client. She has a duty to use her best efforts to win the case. This means that she has to bite and scratch and kick and scream until she has convinced the trier of fact that her position on a given point is correct. In essence this means that she must be able to argue a given proposition eloquently and effectively; that she must be able to spot the weaknesses of her opponent and exploit them to her advantage. In this sense, the training that we get in law school is good, and it should be encouraged. . . . However, the problem arises when this frame of mind carries over to other interests. I definitely want to be a lawyer and a good one but I will also have a family and friends who will have other interests and who will expect me to be responsive to their needs and sorrows, their joys and happiness.

Another student expressed this concern, not with respect to family and friends only, but with respect to other people in law school. He was, in other words, specifically concerned about climate:

> It is easy to bury your love and let your selfish nature possess your actions, especially in the law school atmosphere. The faces we put on for those we want to impress are faces that fulfill a need in each of us. But this need can be fulfilled in many other ways which speak of love and not selfishness. I hope that my life will speak as strongly. It is up to me and it is something I must do. Can I? These heavy thoughts are a real drag, unless one is able to laugh at oneself and make light of those things that others consider heavy. . . .

In much the same mood, a third student said:

> If there's one thing I really hope never to lose, that's my humanity. Law to me at the present time tends to deal with problems only after they have occurred. Why must all disagreements be settled in court? This only brings out the worst in people. . . . Different situations in law school really frighten me. It seems that many people are losing their sense of humanity and becoming very—shall I say—professional in their attitudes toward life and what part love will play in their lives. The logical, rational lawyer appears to be gaining among my classmates. I wonder what my own reaction will be. I fear that perhaps my own weaknesses will draw me into a pattern similar to theirs. I am hoping that I can keep my head together. Do I want to fit in? I presently do not want to fit in if [lawyers] are so warped as to lose a human perspective. That is not what my life has led me

> toward. If need be, a removal from their reality may help me to restore a reality for myself. . . .

All of these were third-year students who were also considering the interpersonal aspects of law practice in a legal counseling course and in a law school clinic. Similar sentiments, with somewhat less of a sense of disappointment in them, are expressed by first-semester students. One of the first-semester students said he hoped law school would motivate him: "I am not much of a go-getter . . . I do what I deem I have to . . . I rarely do much more, which is not all good. I will work as hard as I have to to reach whatever goal I'm shooting for—and I do have decent goals." And then he indicated feelings which at first seem contradictory—that he was uninterested in working hard enough to be the best, but that he had come to law school because he felt he had to learn to work effectively: "One of these goals is not to become the best lawyer I can possibly be. That would detract from a more important goal—to become the best person I can possibly be. . . . I see a career in law as a way to force myself to overcome the laziness that keeps me from acting. I must get beyond the armchair stage, the theorizing without implementing, testing. Law will—at the very least—encourage me to work toward doing something about what I think in the coziness by my bedroom desk."

Both of these themes—a desire to be made efficient and fulfilled in altruism and a desire to avoid emotional retooling in law school—appear in remarks from other first-semester students: "As one of the few who have little desire to make a fortune or a mark (since either usually implies inordinate amounts of time and work), I wonder if one could be a lawyer and live 'outside the law' to some degree. I've seen a number of people sacrifice everything for their jobs—and in the end they find out they really didn't like the jobs."

Another:

> When I was younger, I wanted to be a concert pianist. I would be inspired by artists who could give their self to an art—who could find through music a giving, a means of expression, communication—an art which would of itself be the source of reward and pleasure. This seemed to bring a dimension to life of which I could never imagine an equal—a richness, a completeness. I hope to bring to the law a measure of that kind of feeling. I'm not quite sure if it can be the same kind of experience. Expression, communication—the reaching out to other people with something to offer that I've nurtured and grown with and given my utmost to develop. It can be a beautiful thing.

These are not in-depth looks at motive and experience; none of our data was that, although some suggested the presence of deep feeling and experience. And even these remarks suggest an aspiration that law school will temper competitiveness with calm rationality. They suggest the law as a way to deal with a disposition to aggression (a lawyer "has to bite and scratch and kick and scream"). A final account, by a third-year student, develops the concern with aggression in somewhat more revealing and personal detail; it is likely, too, that emphasis on order and controlled aggression has much to do with this law student's choice of career:

> This year the students in the law school formed a football team again. I thought it would be a good idea to play against the team from the undergraduate residence hall where I am a resident assistant. The game started okay and then progressively got worse. Because the players from the residence hall started getting tough, then the ones from the law school followed suit. From tough it went to rough and then to playing dirty: hitting kidneys, stepping on someone's feet, hitting in the face and so forth.
>
> As I saw and felt this I was completely shaken—physical aggression by adults has always done that to me, not only because of the violence, but because somehow it is very sad that adult, "civilized" human beings would become so violent with one another, and because aggression begets aggression. After the game, and for hours, I was completely drained, physically and mentally.
>
> I have had a problem with aggression, and having to accept it, and yet at the same time finding a way to control my anger. As a child I remember being angry or having a temper fit. My first memory of having a temper fit is when I was 12 and separated from my parents. I was living with my brother and sister in a temporary foster home. I assumed the role of protecting them, and became very angry very easily. This anger was violent sometimes—in fact, most of the time—even physical. Even though I know that we are just human and cannot achieve perfection here on earth it is still hard for me to accept anger and aggression.
>
> I think I have been able to accept imperfection in other areas of my life, but, because I have not been able to accept my anger and aggression, I have a terrible fear of aggression. I get very upset when I see aggression by other people, aggression which is directed at me or at someone else. I guess I am just afraid of violence. I enjoy competition, but I still haven't mastered how to deal with anger. It is true that when I'm away from home I don't get angry, usually, because I have my happy-go-lucky personality, and I just don't let people get to me. But when I'm home I get rattled more easily, since I care more about it, and my family also knows how to get to me.

> There are still times when I get physical—rarely, now. I sometimes punch a pillow, but somehow I feel silly, and immature, afterwards. I think it is not mature to express anger that way, but it's better than expressing anger in angry words and I feel better afterwards—because it is not mature to shout. Also I think that I should argue my points logically and rationally, but I never do, and that's why I never argue about things I really care about—religion, politics, way of life—with my family or friends. I have to express my anger some way. If I don't, if I swallow it, it's bad for my body, because I literally shake and get an upset stomach.
>
> I know in my mind that it is okay to have angry feelings, and that it is good to express them, but somehow, emotionally, I have not been able to accept this. I have from my religion, or somewhere, the idea that one has to strive for perfection. Even though I know that we are just human and cannot achieve perfection on earth.

2. *Students come to law school, to some significant extent, out of an interest in justice.* "Interest in justice" sometimes means a theoretical, to-each-his-due ordering of human affairs. It sometimes means a reform of economic and social injustices that have come to concern students during their college years. The interest, in other words, is not always clearly idealistic.

First-year students often state that concern with justice or social change (or both) is the principal reason they chose the legal profession. And they often exhibit considerable stubbornness about it. "Almost everyone I talk to tells me that I will be coerced into being a private attorney in a firm, but I doubt it. I am not the kind of individual who would fit very well in a large law office. . . . I want to do something socially relevant and that is it."

Another: "I came to law school because I had the feeling that I had some kind of commitment to justice . . . some kind of sharing among people; a distribution of rights; a means of working out a way for individuals to live together, where each is entitled to certain privileges on the same footing with others."

"But," he said, "I'm beginning to feel that perhaps this is all a beautiful illusion." His disillusionment is common, even in the first semester. Some of it is traceable to information about the way the law works. One student, for example, reported a conversation with her property teacher: "The gist of our conversation was that the law in many aspects is more form than anything else. It would be easy to convert it and make it employable by a layman, but that would ruin the value (or at least hamper the earning power) of the professional lawyer . . . I think there are limits to this caste system. I'm an infant in the study of law, but even a child recognizes extreme dangers."

"I have seen what law school means," a third-year student said, "and it frightens me. People lose whatever humanity they possessed, or allow it to become suppressed so they can make out." Another commented on a prayer that is posted in the law library at Notre Dame, which disapproves of competence without compassion: "It's impossible. There is no competence without compassion. There is technical or mechanical expertise here maybe, but no competence." And a third-year student said he felt angry and depressed at his inability to learn, in three years, how to be personally helpful to his clients. "In the end, what difference does it make if someone knows what your fears are or how you feel about them? It's as if you can only know and communicate with someone up to a point. The rest all lies outside another's grasp. I get a kind of monotonous and sickening feeling when I think about that. I want to leave."

3. *Students in law school are verbalizers and order producers whose altruism directs them toward using these skills for suasion and implementation to benefit people.* As one student reflected, "Did More ever consider what is opium for the lawyers? Law is order. Lawyers are orderly. It was so structured and yet probably unnoticed by them, more likely ignored." Another student made the observation in more personal terms. "I'm expecting law to provide the framework my legalistic bent requires for social action. I need to see results." A third student savored the emotional gratification he found in verbal expression: "I did take my first law school exams and I felt good about them. Even if I am totally off base, I was extremely fascinated by the words and thoughts which were flowing from my hands through my fingers and onto my paper."

These students seem to be saying that law school is an exercise in intellectual ordering, but they seem also to fear that it does not order the affairs of real people in a real world. Words and concepts are helpful, even essential, but they tend to become a study in themselves, detachable and ultimately detached from experience. They no longer serve to aid understanding; they become feats of engineering in their own right. They tend to be appreciated for their casuistic qualities. In effect, words that originally attached to feelings and meaningful experiences become part of a linguistic game, and it is the game—detached, aloof, and at times irrelevant—that is meant to speak for real experience.

This beguiling sense of order and solution appealed to and bothered one student. "It finally seems like my law classes are all beginning to fit together. But the one thing that disturbs me is that there seems to be an almost total disregard for finding the truth. Criminal law seems to be little more than finding tricks to get off admitted violators. In contracts, through the guise of 'implied promise,' the courts do whatever they feel like and enforce any promise they want to. There seems to be a common disregard for the responsibility to operationalize a moral code into real-life predicaments." Another student was more succinct: "You may hammer a square client into a round legal solution, or concentrate on classically legal solutions while ignoring 'nonlegal' solutions. The second is also very necessary. You can have all the good intentions in the world, but if your 'estate plan' is snuffed out by the rule against perpetuities what the hell good is it?"

Students, and lawyers, continue to use words and phrases and concepts as both opiate and salvation. They become skilled at words as they pursue their own needs for explanation and order, but it is often not the order of real experience that they have learned to become concerned with. The process caught up with one third-year student who expressed his self-concern in a reflective observation: "I suppose one could rationalize your actions one way or another, yet I still wonder about what things will be like five or ten years from now. It just sometimes seems that one learns to jump through different hoops without really questioning what you're doing or why you're doing it. Maybe the philosophy is wrong. Maybe we just have been doing it for so long that we keep thinking up different legal opiates to soothe our consciences. It's times like this that I really worry about my competency to stand as someone's counsel."

4. *Students perceive before law school that the practice of law is a professional service for people. They come expecting to learn skills for interpersonal professional relationships, and they are frustrated at finding none. But those few who enter into skills training in human relations believe that training in people skills is possible in legal education.* Someone who was about to graduate from law school said:

> I think lawyers tend to be more egotistical as a professional group than any other profession except physicians, and that makes it difficult for them to face their own limitations. I think lawyers, as a result, are very result- or solution-oriented. I have come to the conclusion that no one is really going to teach me how to behave as a lawyer, because no one really knows how a lawyer should behave. I don't think I'll be satisfied with my own practice of the law unless I can make more of an effort to make my client rely on himself, even though this may be contrary to my own egotistical needs.

This student and many of her classmates perceive interpersonal relations in law practice as the lawyer's exploitation of client dependence. "What is it about our profession," one of them said, "that forces a non-lawyer who is talking about lawyers to embellish the facts? What is wrong with the good old folksy telling it like it is? Is it because people are suspicious of lawyers, or possibly that they feel they are in an inferior position?" There is a fatalism in this reaction—as if interpersonal skills are not learned in law school because it is impossible to learn them:

> Being nice to people many times can be hypocritical. As principled as I want to be, in reality I see that I cannot take the stance I would prefer. Society demands certain attitudes, reactions, etc., from certain types of people—as a lawyer, businessman, or whatever. I seem to have no choice. Perhaps it is just me reacting to my legal education (but my education accentuates a careless indifference to people). If treating another kindly more often means feeling sorry for him, rather than seeing him as a fellow, an equal human being. Personal involvement and the law don't seem to mix. If you want to be good you must be indifferent. I have yet to find myself in a situation where emotion has done anything for me other than to scramble my sometimes good judgment.

Another student:

> I find in myself the tendency not to really listen to what someone is telling me. When I reply to what the other person has said, I find that I am not being responsive: I have not really read what the other is saying. I think I know why. I feel I have been so concerned about what I will say next—or so concerned at whether what I will say will sound good—that when it comes time for me to respond I really can't, because I haven't listened. It's sad. I recognize now that this is a substantial reason for not being able to get close to people. My consciousness of this problem is, though, helping me to come out of it. But it makes me very sad when I think of the way my inability to get close, and to listen, has affected those with whom I have tried to have meaningful relationships. Not listening is part of it. There's another part, too. I find that often I say things not because I really feel strongly about them, but because I think they are what the other person wants to hear. I have thought about this problem, too, and I think it arises from my own strong desire to be accepted by the other person, or by a fear that he will reject me. I don't have enough confidence to think that other people will accept me for what I really am, and, as a result, try to be something that I am not.

Another:

> Two practicing lawyers talked to us about counseling. One said he thinks lawyers have no business counseling. I think he has a real problem. He came on much too forcefully to really believe what he was saying. I dislike his saying that he tells the client what to do

> and what he wants. But, then, maybe that's how you have to do it. My experience doesn't give me a right to scrutinize him, and his approach. He also upset me. He sounds like someone who should broadcast for Radio Free Europe. I got the idea that he wanted everyone in the room to agree with him, and that he wasn't willing to give up until they did. Maybe he walks on a narrow tightrope.

First-year students have hopes for interpersonal competence, without as much disillusionment over their ability to learn it, or legal education's ability to offer it to them: "I want a small town personal sort of practice where I can be not only an attorney but a friend. This sounds rather idealistic, and I know that there is no way I can be a 'friend,' in the true meaning of the word, to all my clients. But I do feel that I can represent my clients and the profession with integrity and effectiveness while at the same time establishing some sort of trusting and concerned relationship with my clients."

"I think a successful lawyer would have to have real empathy for his clients, to understand their needs and to explain legal situations," a classmate said. And then he doubted his ability to perform at that level: "On the other hand, when a lawyer is actually working he would be better to be rather cold. Empathy should be part of his motivation, but he would probably work better without that motivation."

The melancholy in these thoughts comes about in part because of insularity in the law school community. It is, in other words, a climate factor more than a curricular factor. One first-year student reported, for instance, that he had joined a study group of his classmates and found it effective and encouraging. A few weeks later he said: "We had to discontinue our regular study group meetings because we were only confusing each other. All four of us have pretty good outlines for all the classes, but when we disagree about a certain point, no one wants to give in and none of us has the time to look up all the things we wonder about. From now on, it's every man on his own—and I think I will be better off."

IMPROVING HUMAN SKILLS IN LEGAL EDUCATION

Skills in human relations are no longer entirely neglected in law schools; many schools now offer elective courses in counseling, and even those that do not are likely to provide relevant printed material, guest lectures, and allusions in substantive classes.

These remarks indicate a sense of hope among students who are studying counseling skills. The hope is that people skills can be learned and, more to the present point, that students feel less disillusioned about their legal education when the school opens their eyes to their own abilities as helpers of people. Here is a student who is beginning to realize that she can be a counselor and that the task calls for dimensions of self-awareness she has not used elsewhere in her legal education.

> This stuff poses a question for me: If I as a counselor am to be effective, I must be able to present myself in such a way that the client feels I am interested in his problem. I want to help him as much as possible. I must be able to convey to him that I am worthy of his trust and confidence and not merely someone who can file papers in his behalf. I suppose that if I want someone to come to me and open himself up, I must be willing to open myself up, in the sense that I care so much about this individual, and convey this to him, that he will have no hesitancy in disclosing himself to me. In order to tear down the barriers between him and me, I must first be willing to tear down some of my own personal barriers.

Students in this situation commonly realize that people skills probably involve a rejection of their lawyer self-images—at least of the superrational, hard-nosed aspects of their self-images:

> It is a simple question of listening and trying to understand what people are really saying to us. This, I am convinced, can only be done if we turn off the lawyer. I think that we should listen in a responsive manner. By that I mean listening so that we can understand what people are saying to us, why they are saying it, and how we should react to their ideas. Listening so that we can receive truth or expressions of another human being. This cannot be done in a frame of mind which is searching for arguments, which is looking for fault, and which is trying to exploit the weaknesses and faults of another's statement.

Another:

> I have realized in the last few years that there is much that goes into building the wombs of comfort and security that each of us longs to live in. Educational institutions are the best. They are wombs-with-a-view. And that is the fault of your law teachers. The primary thrust of legal education as I have experienced it has been directed at learning the naked law. No human issues have been involved. Rather, we have been trained to apply *X* law when a *Y* problem has been presented. There has been very little attention given to avoiding courtroom conflict. We have been trained only in terms of the ultimate result, adjudication in a court of law.
>
> People generally fear and shy away from anything they do not understand and lawyers are probably more prone to react this way

> than the average person. Then, too, law students find it difficult to talk to people as people—there is a need to always talk at or about something. At this rate, it would probably be difficult to get students to just talk on their own about how they see themselves as lawyers. When we do talk about our future, our statements seem so fixed and said only to see what reactions they can cause in others, and the others respond with answers, not their true feelings, but to see what reaction they will receive. This perhaps comes from the fact that no one is sure of what general direction we're headed in.

Another:

> Once some meaningful relationship has been established, feelings can be expressed and exchanged and be transformed, sort of, from what were once harsh judgments. The relationship seems to be the key. Sometimes I think that a client feels that he has to prove his value to his lawyer. He feels that he has to prove that his problem is a serious one, one that merits my consideration. Perhaps the difference may lie in whether or not the lawyer feels she is dealing with a client or a customer. Webster defines a "customer" as a person who buys. He defines a "client" as a dependent; the word comes from the Latin meaning to lean, as, basically, one leaning on another for protection. For myself, I feel a greater awareness of others as human beings and a greater awareness of myself as a human being in relation to others. Before we started going into this stuff, I felt very cocky. I thought I was very concerned with others. I now feel that I have a long way to go.

Several students in this situation (third-year students in a class devoted to counseling skills) reported in some detail on experience they had with real clients in the law school clinic. Two of these experiences tend to demonstrate that interpersonal skills are an important part of what law students seek from their education and to indicate as well that advertent attention to counseling skills is possible and profitable, both in terms of preparation for the profession and in terms of effective response to student expectations.

First case:

> I met with my 25-year-old client at what I believed would be our final session together. In preparation for this meeting, I had spent nearly a dozen hours preparing the several legal forms necessary to file for a guardianship, as well as researching to familiarize myself with the existing law and terminology of that area. All that was required at this point was the notarization of several signatures. When the time had arrived for the signatures to be placed on the prepared forms, my client informed me of a complete change of desire since

my earlier conversation with her. My work had been all but completely negated. I felt a little sick inside; a little anger—well, perhaps more than a little anger, a little depression, and a lot of frustration. I realized that it was a tense moment for my client. That is, her refusal to sign the necessary forms which I had so painstakingly drawn placed her, in her perception, I believe, in a defensive position with her attorney—me.

In order to avoid any more tension than that which had already found its way into our counseling room, I smiled and rather reassuringly said, "No problem." It was from this point that we proceeded to really talk with one another. My client let me be a counselor. As a result a number of her heretofore secret reservations came to light. At the close of our meeting, I asked my client to think about what we had discussed and talk it over with her family. I told her I would contact her after the weekend. After this period of reflection, we were able to work everything out, and to everyone's agreement. Writing this incident on paper, though I have been skeletal in its description, causes me to wonder how I handled my role prior to my client's refusal to sign the forms. I wonder if I took too much for granted (i.e., assumed that there should be no real questions or reservations about the papers I had prepared). I wonder also if I had been too egocentric—after all, I felt that I had done a good job preparing the case—at least the mechanical aspects of the case.

Second:

It really bothers me whether or not I'll be able to distinguish a lie from the truth. I am the kind of person who is quickly able to accept what a person says as being true, and I sometimes, later, find out that he was just giving me a line. It takes me a long time to ever trust that person again. When I was working in the prosecutor's office, people would come in and give me a song and a dance, and I didn't realize it was a song and dance, and I would almost immediately believe them, I got all upset with the attorneys in the office, who would ignore what these people said: "So what?" And I asked myself: "What the hell are they getting paid for?" The I found out that there was a regular crew of people who come in and lie. Not a word of what they say is true. I just got sucked in by them. So I learned a lesson. But what bothers me is whether I'll become so hardened and insensitive that when someone comes in with a legitimate problem, and is really levelling with me, I won't be able to spot it. I know there is no answer to the problem and that I'm going to get burned a few times, and that I'll learn from experience, but I only hope that I don't learn too well, that I will be able to retain some of this idealism.

STRATEGY FOR A HUMANISTIC CLIMATE

Humanistic climate can be sought through a strategy of acceptance. The accepting climate is a theoretical notion advanced in a classic subcategory of counseling literature by the late, eminent psychotherapist Carl Rogers (1972). Rogers believed that most maladjustments in human behavior trace to feelings of guilt or disapproval. His cure was a kind of psychotherapeutic allopathy: The patient (Rogers called him a client) contains within himself all of the resources necessary for cure. The task of the therapist is to create an atmosphere—a climate—in which this tendency for cure can operate. This idea can be usefully borrowed for a discussion of institutional climate—law school climate, in this case. The analogy can also be explored in the even more specialized literature of "human potential" groups. Rogerians believe these groups, which they call "encounter groups," work best when all structure is avoided; leaders of Rogerian groups are consequently called "facilitators." The other school of group work, tracing roughly from the use of psychotherapeutic groups led by psychiatrists, prescribes a more or less manipulated environment.

The Rogerian ideal in a law school would be a climate of acceptance and of individual responsibility for behavior. The idea is to convey to students a sense of validation—a sense that their instincts toward altruism or competition or oral aggression are not likely to encounter disapproval from other students or from the law faculty. Adapting Rogers, one could talk about this sort of climate as involving the following:

1. *unconditional positive regard*: a communication to the student, in some believable way, that he is valued as a person, regardless of his views and habits:
2. *empathy*: a communication to the student, from someone she regards as significant in the law school, that others know how she feels and are able to share her feelings without any necessity to approve or disapprove of them; and
3. *congruence*: the impression that professors and classmates are healthy, growing, well-integrated people—people who do not need to exploit or manipulate others.

This sort of climate would be—would have to be—person centered in a radical and deliberate way. It represents ancient community values that virtually everyone in a law school community acknowledges, if only sentimentally. Scripture expressed them in a Hebraic context when it said, "Let us be concerned for each other, to stir a response in love and good works" (Hebrews 10:24). Even the smallest sort of effort toward an educational regimen based on acceptance would no doubt change the climate of any law school. Any significant growth toward an accepting climate would produce a school unlike any other in the history of legal education—a school without Socratic teaching (because it would refuse to mold people by disapproving of them), a place where students would explore their own ideas until they themselves had evaluated and changed or integrated these codes, an interpersonal atmosphere in which each person has a stake in the success of each of the others. The radical impact an accepting climate would have is probably best illustrated in the remarks of the law students quoted above, about the climate they find in law schools as they are. It would probably astonish most people in law schools to know that these ideals actually operate, advertently, in many successful law firms.

10

Corporate Compliance Education: Where Are Business Schools?

W. Richard Sherman

If it can be said that law schools produce "adversaries" (Bok 1983), then business schools produce "competitors." All their lives, business students have been competing—competing to get into quality schools so that they can compete to get high grades in their college courses so that they can compete for good job offers and/or for placement into prestigous MBA programs so that they can compete for even more attractive job offers. This is not to say that other college students are not competitive—far from it. But if there is one characteristic that separates the business student from his or her counterpart in the liberal arts and sciences, it is this sense of being in a competition in which the ultimate scoring system is defined in what are essentially monetary terms. Money is the name of the game—not so much for what it can buy, but because that is how success is measured.

Not surprisingly, the business curriculum reinforces this focus on the dollars-and-cents aspects of life. Courses in accounting, finance, and marketing are all primarily taught from and based on a perspective in which costs and benefits can be quantified and expressed in monetary terms for rational decision making—*viz.*, for the maximization of profits. Even the "softer" disciplines of management and human resources (often called the "touchy-feely" fields of business) are becoming more and more quantitative and statistical. Indeed, one common trend throughout the continually evolving business curriculum is this quantification, with more courses in mathematics, statistics, and quantitative methods being inserted at its core. One colleague at a major state university recently remarked, only somewhat facetiously, that his suggestion at his school's next curriculum committee meeting would be to completely eliminate all business majors. Instead, all would-be business students would major in mathematics and simply have a minor in management or marketing or accounting or finance.

What business faculty and students share is a belief that most things can be reduced to numbers. Perhaps the decision models we currently use are not sufficiently sophisticated to incorporate all the variables, but given time, an answer in dollars and cents will lead us to an optimal decision—or so they believe. Unlike many a liberal arts major who views numbers as hard, pointy things that can hurt, the business student takes comfort in the seeming exactness that numerical solutions provide. It is from this number-dominated backdrop that proposals for more efficient and effective corporate compliance must be judged.

THE BUSINESS CURRICULUM: A STATUS REPORT

Not all business schools are the same—just as not all liberal arts colleges or all law schools or all medical schools are the same. But there is a far greater congruence of curricula and objectives between and among business schools than among other pieces of the academic puzzle. The cause of the similarities among business schools is in large measure the influence of a single, almost universally accepted arbiter of excellence in business education: the American Assembly of Collegiate Schools of Business (AACSB). AACSB accreditation is the most eagerly sought affirmation of a school's quality. If a business school does not already have AACSB accreditation, then more than likely it is in the process of planning for (perhaps "hoping for" would be a better description) eventual AACSB accreditation.

As part of its accrediting procedures and standards, the AACSB sets guidelines for adequate resources—computer facilities, libraries, doctorally qualified faculty, and so on. And it also sets standards for the business curriculum itself—the so-called "common body of knowledge" (CBK).

As one would expect from an organization created by, for, and of business educators, the AACSB's CBK contains a large dose of the quantitative stuff: accounting; quantitative methods; management information systems, including computer applications; and the like. But the AACSB also requires that at least one year of work be included in an accreditable school's course of instruction to provide "a background of the economic and legal environment as it pertains to profit and/or nonprofit organizations along with ethical considerations and social and political influences as they affect such organizations" (AACSB 1989, 32).

It is in meeting this requirement that business schools will address the issue of corporate compliance, if they address it at all. The courses that most frequently delve into the economic, legal, and social environment in which modern business and the corporation function carry titles such as Business and Society, Business Law, Legal Environment of Business, Business Policy, and/or Social Responsibility. In these courses, students learn about the ever-present shadow of government regulation: environmental protection, prohibitions on uses of insider information, restrictions on anticompetitive behavior by corporations, health and safety requirements in the workplace, and so on.

BUSINESS ETHICS

The most recent emphasis added to these courses (and to the business curriculum in general) is a consideration of ethical issues in business. In part a reaction to the perceived amoral attitudes of business students and practitioners,[1] as well as to such highly publicized "yuppie" crimes as insider trading, this focus has been met with a good degree of ambivalence. On the one hand, ethics do not fit into a numerical model very easily. Given the bias of accounting, finance, and other quantitatively oriented faculty, resistance to yet another intrusion into their traditional courses should have been expected. This resistance often takes the form of arguing that ethics are by their very nature personal, subjective, value-laden, and value-ridden. How, then, can a meaningful discussion and a well-reasoned decision take place?

In one of the more thoughtful considerations of the area of business ethics, Thomas W. Dunfee (1987, 386) reviewed and countered the principal arguments against the teaching of ethics, arriving at what he calls the "intermediate principles of business ethics." Using these principles as a foundation for the analysis of business decisions, professors, students, and business persons can all address ethical problems within some mutually agreed on framework for better appreciation, if not ultimate solution, of the conflicts involved.

Yet there are still many professors who feel uncomfortable with the prospect of dealing with ethics in their courses. At one Catholic university, a rather heated debate arose over a proposal to include the Ethics Resource Center's video *It's Up to You* (1987) on management accountants' ethical dilemmas in the undergraduate introductory managerial accounting course. Arguments ranged from the concern that the ethical issues depicted in the scenarios would be "over our students' heads" to the sweetly ironic fear that the students would cheat on the written assignment that would be required as part of the course. A pervasive concern seems to be that the professor would be seen as "preaching" his or her own ethical perspective—something that may be acceptable in a theology or philosophy class, but not in the business school.

On the other hand, who in his or her right mind would say that ethics have no place in business education and practice? This would be tantamount to coming out against God, Mom, and apple pie. In many ways, ethics have become big business in and of themselves. Harvard Business School received a $30 million gift to incorporate ethics into its world-renowned MBA curriculum (Byrne and Beam 1987). A similar direction, under the corporate sponsorship of Exxon, has been taken to integrate ethics into the graduate coursework at the University of Pennsylvania's Wharton School (Dunfee 1986). Thoughtful and well-prepared videos highlight situations where businesspersons and professionals encounter ethical dilemmas [see Homer and Stenek (1989) for a bibliography of available audiovisual aids]. The Ethics Resource Center and the international accounting and consulting firm of Arthur Anderson & Company, in addition to preparing videos for use both in college classrooms and in continuing professional education programs, conduct seminars that focus on the side of business that cannot be reduced to a "bottom line."

Whatever form the instruction takes, whether taught as a separate course such as Social Responsibility or sprinkled throughout various courses, ethics have clearly become part of the business curriculum. In a 1988 survey, the Ethics Resource Center found that 90 percent of the business schools responding to its questionnaire included ethics in their required coursework.

CORPORATE COMPLIANCE—BEYOND ETHICS

While the introduction of ethics into the curriculum is laudable, it really is not what corporate compliance is about. In a sense compliance is beyond ethics—not because compliance is a higher form of ethical behavior, but because compliance is a different issue altogether. To be compliant is not necessarily to be ethical.[2] Nevertheless, there is an obvious interplay between ethics and compliance. In many cases government regulation is designed to prohibit or constrain unethical behavior. Even where the ethical dimension is absent, compliance with regulation shares the problem of ethical behavior in that it can rarely be expressed in terms that business students and faculty can readily appreciate: profits and losses.

When corporate compliance is considered in business education, it is treated as merely another variable to be added into the equation. Most frequently it is considered just another cost of doing business—and then a cost that should be minimized or avoided, if possible. As one professor writes, while we do "try, to some degree, to teach interpersonal skills, teamwork skills, negotiating skills, and political skills . . . we don't do a very good job . . . because their mastery requires a lot of practice, and most business schools have been designed without practice fields" (Leavitt 1989, 40). It is much easier to simply try to insert compliance with government regulation and its attendant costs into an analytical model as yet another constraint or, worse, to note its existence and then ignore it because it cannot be reduced to some number.

THE SELLING OF INTERACTIVE COMPLIANCE

For it to have any meaningful impact, the concept of interactive compliance must be "sold" to business faculties, students, and graduates as a more effective and efficient way of living with and prospering under government regulation. In short, given the nature of the beast that is the business school, this selling must show how being compliant makes good business sense—as measured in dollars and cents.

Is it to a corporation's advantage to be compliant? On a fairly basic level, if compliance relieves the corporation of the fines and penalties of regulatory violations, sure. But this may not be enough of an incentive. The "stick" mentality has its limitations, for it is not the severity of the punishment that makes a sanction effective; it is the certainty that the punishment will be imposed. In the area of corporate compliance, detection and consequential sanction are anything but certain. So there must be a better way. This is where interactive compliance comes into play.

THE ACCOUNTING MODEL

An exact parallel to the interactive corporate compliance model already exists in the area of corporate financial reporting. Perhaps the quintessential example of the compliance situation is the requirement that a company's financial statements be prepared in conformity with generally accepted accounting principles (GAAP). The compliance investigation is conducted not by a government official, but by a highly trained, independent professional—the certified public accountant (CPA). The CPA conducting the audit examines the corporate records in order to express his or her opinion on the "fairness" of the financial statements. These audits are expensive—in terms of time, effort, aggravation, and, maybe most importantly, money. But the corporation can reduce the costs of the audit by engaging in interactive compliance.

In the financial reporting sphere, interactive compliance takes the form of an internal control structure. All companies have an internal control mechanism that is designed to safeguard the company's assets and give some assurance that the accounting numbers being spewed out of the accounting system are reasonably reliable.[3] However, not all internal control systems are created equal. Some are well designed, manned by certified internal auditors (or CIAs, a fitting acronym) who report directly to an independent internal audit committee, which is outside the "line of fire" and influence of management. Others are considerably weaker. Clearly, the stronger the internal control structure is, the more expensive it will be to create, implement, and maintain. So where is the payoff?

The first advantage of a strong system of internal control is found in the enhanced quality of the information being provided to executives, managers, investors, and other users. However, while this advantage is unquestionably important, it is blunted somewhat by the fact that it is difficult to put a price tag on the improvement of information quality. For those who like to "crunch numbers," as accountants do, the cost-benefit trade-off is uncertain at best. More "selling" is required before the corporation will "buy" into this.

A second advantage is a bit more quantifiable. The stronger the internal control system, the less likely that defalcations and other employee misdeeds will go undetected. Still, the actual savings cannot be calculated with any precision, and even if they could, the total dollar amounts involved may not be that significant. As with the first advantage, it would be difficult to justify the additional costs of a stronger system of internal control in terms of dollars-and-cents benefits. To make matters worse in trying to draw an analogy, neither of these advantages carries over to the broader field of corporate compliance. However, a third advantage of a strong system of internal control—the reduced cost of compliance—does.

One of the first tasks of the CPA making an audit is to evaluate the client's internal control structure. The stronger the system, the more the CPA can rely on the numbers it produces. The more the CPA can rely on the numbers, the less extensive the investigation he or she has to do in terms of performing "substantive" tests (i.e., tests for the accuracy of the dollar amounts contained in any account). The fewer the substantive tests, the less costly the audit—in terms of time, effort, and money. This is where a company's internal control structure can pay for itself. Add to this the somewhat intangible value of enhanced information quality and the prevention of theft or misuse, and a corporation has all the incentive it needs to buy the concept and practice of interactive compliance.

This is exactly the kind of selling that already takes place in business education. Throughout the accounting curriculum, from the introductory course in financial accounting through principles of auditing and into courses in accounting information systems, the advantages of internal control are extolled. Without conscious effort accounting students have bought into the need for and benefits derived from this type of interactive compliance, just as their professors have bought into this idea before them. And it is this appreciation of the virtues of interactive compliance, however narrowly applied, that the students take out with them to the work place.

A similar model of internal control in the area of compliance could be developed and sold in courses throughout the business curriculum. Just as the interactive compliance between the CIA and the independent, external CPA can result in substantial cost savings, so, too, can the interactive compliance between corporate officers and regulatory agents. Real-world examples already exist. For example, in teaching business strategy, management professors could point to the successful partnership of corporations and government in Japan. This cooperative, interactive relationship extends far beyond mere financial support into areas of regulation, and it accounts in part for the extraordinary success of "Japan Inc." in international trade.

In Legal Environment and in Business and Society courses, the reality of government regulation should be presented less as a constraint and more as an assurance of freer competition and social good. Not that this will be an easy task; a longstanding bias must be overcome on both sides of the debate. But rather than narrowly viewing government as yet another "competitor," business students should be exposed to the potential opportunities to interact with government agencies as a safeguard that all competition can take place on a level playing field. Rather than trying to change the nature of business students, these courses and their instructors can sell interactive compliance by appealing to those students' competitive instincts—by showing how such a system can be in their best interest by being in their corporation's best interest.

It may also be time to develop a new type of professional—a certified compliance officer—whose training would necessarily begin in his or her college days. A hallmark of this professional would be the ability to be independent without being adversarial. Such a professional would have a place in both the corporate and the government spheres, mirroring the situation that presently exists in accounting with CIAs and CPAs.

THE MARKETING TOOL

A record of "good" compliance, one of the underpinnings of interactive compliance, should also be viewed as a potentially rewarding marketing tool. A recent survey by Greenpeace found that 77 percent of all consumers base their purchasing decisions on the environmental records of the companies making the products. While perhaps oversimplifying consumers' motivations, this finding does indicate that a company can gain a competitive advantage from its compliance. In short, an exceptional compliance record does create some "value added" to the company's products.

Product differentiation ranging from the use of the "recycled" symbol on paper products to the establishment of a consumer safety board can create a public image that makes compliance profitable. These strategies should be introduced and emphasized in the marketing strategy component of any number of business courses—Business Policy, Strategic Management, and, of course, several offerings by the marketing department.

The pricing of a company's products would also be affected. With a system of interactive compliance, one could expect transaction costs to be reduced due to greater trust and lesser fear that unfair advantage will be gained by those who are "reluctant compliers."[4] This would be the case whether or not government agencies "sweetened" the deal by reducing the number of compliance investigations undertaken against those companies with a history of good compliance or granted some other preferential treatment to "known compliers" (Sigler and Murphy 1988, 149–51). Such savings could be reflected in lower prices, thereby adding to the company's competitive advantage.

By including these payoffs in the discussion of government regulation and its impact on marketing and business decisions, business professors can help change the attitudes of a new generation of corporate executives who will be the ones who can make interactive compliance a reality.

DISCRETIONARY COMPLIANCE

One area of business planning that offers the greatest opportunity for interactive compliance is that involving discretionary compliance. Silverstein (1987) has identified various stages of management's responsiveness to social demands and has linked them to Ackerman's (1973) zone of discretion spectrum.

In Type 1 situations, where there is a relatively high degree of regulation (and consequently relatively little discretion), corporations respond to social demands based on legal requirements. This is perhaps the most common scenario of corporate compliance today. In such a setting it is doubtful that either the enforcement agency or the corporate compliance department would be receptive to close cooperation and interaction with one another. They are set up as adversaries and will continue to play out their roles.

In Type 2 situations, on the other hand, relatively greater discretion (and relatively less regulation) exists, and corporations are more willing and able to act with "enlightened self-interest." They will seek to be more cooperative since they can see how such cooperation can be profitable. Companies and entire industries may even propose additional regulation in an effort to stave off more restrictive measures. It is in precisely such a context that interactive compliance would seem most beneficial.

Once again, accounting practices offer an illustration of this discretionary compliance. Every country has its own version of GAAP. While U.S. and British GAAP require a tremendous amount of information regarding the financial affairs of a publicly traded company, this is not the norm throughout the rest of the world. In point of fact in international financial reporting there is something of an information vacuum. Even such highly developed countries as Germany and Switzerland require fairly minimal financial disclosure for many of their native companies. Historically many of these non-U.S. corporations have actively opposed the more complete and detailed disclosure required of companies trading in the United States, arguing that such disclosure would be giving away company secrets. For example, if the company's sales by geographic region were made public (as required under U.S. GAAP), then competitors would have some of the critical information regarding potential markets or lines of supplies, thereby enabling them to gobble up these sales or lines of production. Much of the financial information is treated as proprietary in nature—and not for public consumption.

However, as capital markets have become increasingly international, geographic boundaries and ideosyncratic national disclosure requirements have become obsolete. If a company wants to compete for the global pool of investment capital, it must be willing to make financial disclosures equal to those of American or British corporations, without regard to the fact that such disclosures are not required by its home country. And this is exactly what has occurred. Foreign corporations have been preparing financial statements with excess disclosure—"excess" in the sense that it is well beyond the information required by their native accounting standards. This discretionary compliance with U.S. GAAP not only has been undertaken in their own self-interest, but also is a virtual necessity for their continued survival in an environment of competitive information.

A similar argument can be made in the area of interactive compliance. If a company is rewarded for its participation in the compliance procedure, be it by preference granted in government contracting or by reduced costs in compliance investigations or by superior public relations, then other companies will be forced to enter into interactive compliance or else find themselves at a competitive disadvantage. As currently taught, business policy and strategy courses largely overlook these zones of discretion and the business sense that interactive compliance can make. This should change—to increase interest, to introduce more realism into the decision model, and to explore otherwise ignored alternatives.

CONCLUSION

Business faculty and their students like to think of themselves as being performance-oriented. Unfortunately, this performance orientation is seen quite narrowly as a competition measured crudely by the maximization of profits. Numbers have become both a scoring device and a fixation. What better example of this than the capstone course offered at the end of most business curricula? In many of these Business Policy courses, students "compete" against one another as fictional firms and are ranked according to their respective bottom lines (or, more accurately, by an "index" or number based on the company's profits). Does it matter that their company is a "good" company, that it willingly complies with environmental standards, provides its workers with a safe and healthy work place, or refuses to engage in discriminatory behavior? These factors do not even enter the "game" because they cannot be reduced to a number. They are not part of the scoring system.

For interactive corporate compliance to gain a receptive audience among business faculties and their students, it must become part of the scoring system; it must be shown to increase revenues or reduce costs. If its benefits cannot be expressed in some tangible form (i.e., be reduced to some dollar amount), interactive compliance will be discounted as yet another proposal that was interesting in theory, but impracticable or unfeasible in actual practice.

In such a setting it is not enough that interactive compliance be offered as one alternative to the existing system of government regulation. Interactive compliance must be "sold" to the students. An argument based on the ethical underpinnings of compliance and of our system of government regulation will not sell. Instead, the competitive advantages that a cooperative and interactive system can bring must be shown and emphasized. Only then will the competitors who now populate our business schools buy it.

NOTES

1. Lane and Schaupp (1989) found that business students have a different, more cynical view of ethics than do students in liberal arts and engineering schools; in a seemingly inconsistent, but perhaps more disturbing, finding, business students perceived themselves as being more concerned with people, social responsibility, and ethics than they thought successful CEOs were (Beggs and Lane 1989). This may mean that however skeptical they may be while in school, business students are even more cynical about what it takes to get to the top of the corporate ladder.

2. It is interesting to note that Dunfee (1987) does include "willing compliance with the law" among his "Intermediate Principles of Business Ethics," adding that "one should comply with the spirit of the law, and not take an adversarial approach based upon a strategy of maximizing noncompliance with the law" (403).

3. Under the Foreign Corrupt Practices Act (15 USCA Sec. 78a, 78n, 78dd-1), companies are required to maintain a system of internal control. The purpose of the inclusion of this accounting requirement in a statute designed to inhibit bribery of foreign officials or political parties is to create an audit trail, thereby enabling enforcement agents to trace the payments through the books of the corporation involved.

4. Dunfee (1987) has made a similar argument as to why it may be profitable to be ethical (403).

11

Political Education Is Necessary to Foster Cooperative Regulatory Enforcement

John T. Scholz

In order for corporations and society to obtain the benefits of interactive corporate compliance, enforcement officials must be willing and able to pursue the kind of cooperative enforcement that would encourage interactive compliance. Regulators have been blamed for much of the inefficient regulations and unreasonable enforcement that interactive compliance is intended to improve. In this chapter I will argue that in the United States, unlike in more authoritarian countries, we generally get the kinds of bureaucrats and inspectors we deserve. The problems associated with enforcement lie to a great degree with us, not the regulators, and the solution will require political education and greater knowledge about how enforcement works.

The growth of regulatory policies in the last two decades has been the result of political demands from consumer, environmental, worker, and community groups that businesses do more in certain areas than market forces demanded of them. The problems associated with regulatory compulsion can be overcome only by convincing *both* these groups and these businesses that political and legal confrontation is less beneficial than more cooperative relationships are.

My argument begins with the basic theme that everyone can be made better off with interactive compliance coupled with cooperative enforcement. To develop this argument, I will begin with a brief review of the reasons that cooperative enforcement works. I then will look at two major political impediments to implementing cooperative enforcement: (1) the lack of support by critical interest groups on both sides of regulatory issues and (2) the most critical problem of developing adequate oversight controls for cooperative enforcement strategies. Basically, the political impediments to more efficient enforcement arise because short-term political interests overshadow the long-term benefits of cooperation.

The final discussion emphasizes the need for convincing demonstrations of the benefits of cooperation, more attention to developing efficient enforcement approaches to specialized problems, and better education of *all* regulatory participants about the long-term benefits of cooperation. Only by convincing *both* proponents and opponents of regulation that the long-term benefits of cooperation are sizable and obtainable can the potential gains in efficiency be realized. The establishment of a small National Academy of Regulatory Enforcement may be the most practical means to this end.

WHY COOPERATIVE ENFORCEMENT WORKS

Evaluations of regulatory effectiveness generally assume that enforcement based on punishment is required to ensure that business firms comply with regulatory standards. Firms will comply to the extent that the value of expected costs of compliance and punishment for noncompliance exceeds the value of expected benefits of noncompliance. Since higher rates of inspection, citation, and penalties should increase the expected costs of noncompliance, higher levels of enforcement should presumably produce more compliance.

While enforcement levels are undoubtedly important to effective enforcement, studies of enforcement agency activities reveal that persuasion and educational activities play at least as great a role as do monitoring and prosecutorial activities in most regulatory enforcement agencies (Bardach and Kagan, 1982; Hawkins and Thomas 1984; Kagan and Scholz 1984; Shover, Lynxwiler, and Clelland 1983), particularly in U.S. agencies prior to the 1960s and outside the United States (Braithwaite, 1985a; Kelman 1982). Even vigorous enforcement programs commonly appear to have such procedures that are not readily explained by the deterrence model of enforcement.

Theoretical studies of enforcement have criticized simple deterrence assumptions from two perspectives. First, the legalistic focus on violations and punishment implicit in the deterrence model ignores the practical problems involved in applying abstract legal rules to the diversity of concrete regulatory situations. Alternative enforcement strategies, including professional (Muir 1977), judicial (Kagan 1978), result-oriented (Nonet and Selznick 1978), normative (Kagan and Scholz 1984; Kelman 1982), reasonable (Bardach and Kagan 1982), and negotiated (Shover, Lynxwiler and Clelland 1983), strategies emphasize the need for flexibility in order to reduce the undesirable and counterproductive consequences that occur when legal rules are enforced with no consideration of mitigating circumstances. Such legalistic enforcement has been observed to increase compliance costs and litigation delays (Shover, Lynxwiler and Clelland 1983), while reducing voluntary compliance and political support for the agency (Kelman 1982).

In a second and more recent focus, game-theoretic models of enforcement illustrate the need to consider more complex interactions between regulated firms and enforcement agencies (Graetz, Reinganum, and Wilde 1986; Greenberg 1984; Reinganum and Wilde 1986; Scholz 1984a). This is particularly true for regulatory enforcement, where the inherent economic inefficiency of regulations combines with the difficulties of monitoring firms and prosecuting violators to make cooperative enforcement particularly attractive. Society as a whole would be better off if the enforcement agency can reduce costly legalistic enforcement in return for extralegal efforts on the part of the regulated firm to work toward the policy objective —in the case of the Occupational Safety and Health Administration (OSHA), to reduce industrial injury and illness rates.

To understand this trade-off and the potential problems involved in using the cooperative strategy, consider a simple game played between the enforcement agency and the regulated firm. The game is similar to one commonly called the "prisoner's dilemma" and is described in detail for the regulatory setting by Scholz (1984a, 1984b). In this game, firms can choose either minimal compliance or flexible compliance, and the agency can choose either maximal enforcement or flexible enforcement. The usual approach to enforcement considers only the deterrence outcome in which the firm always chooses minimal compliance and the agency always chooses maximal enforcement. In this outcome, as noted before, the firm's level of compliance minimizes the costs of compliance, expected penalties, and legal costs net of any benefits gained by the firm from improved safety. The agency always chooses maximal enforcement that imposes penalties for all detected violations and requires all violations to be abated, regardless of cost or suitability for the firm's particular safety problems. This equilibrium is inevitably wasteful because of the inherent economic inefficiency associated with regulatory standards plus the unproductive costs associated with monitoring compliance and prosecuting violators.

In most regulatory enforcement arenas, an alternative voluntary compliance outcome exists that would be preferred by both firm and agency and that would reduce some of the social inefficiencies associated with regulation. The agency could reduce its monitoring and prosecution costs if firms would always choose flexible compliance, a level of compliance that produces greater social benefits than does minimal compliance. Firms would prefer flexible compliance over minimal compliance as long as agency officials respond with flexible enforcement, overlooking minor technical violations in recognition of the firm's extralegal safety efforts to reduce greater hazards not directly addressed in regulations (Bardach and Kagen 1982; Sigler and Murphy 1988). Such flexibility would allow a firm to tackle its worst health and safety hazards with the most efficient methods available, rather than spending money to comply with safety standards that are less important and inefficient in the firm's particular situation. The voluntary compliance outcome provides both firm and agency with the mutual rewards of flexible compliance combined with flexible enforcement.

While firm and agency both prefer voluntary compliance to deterrence, they would be even better off in the short run if each one took advantage of the other's flexibility. If the firm chooses minimal compliance and the agency chooses flexible enforcement, the firm may avoid most or all compliance costs and produce little of the safety improvement desired by the agency. Similarly, if the agency chooses maximal enforcement and the firm chooses flexible compliance, the firm loses more than full compliance costs, and the agency gains greater safety than full compliance alone would bring. The first outcome is associated with the social costs of capture by regulated firms, and the second with the social costs of harassment by an overzealous agency. Both outcomes are less efficient and therefore less socially desirable than voluntary compliance; yet both present temptations to either firm or agency. If the agency knew the firm's choice prior to committing itself, it could simply respond with flexible enforcement when the firm chose flexible compliance. However, flexible enforcement saves monitoring costs by reducing the frequency and intrusiveness of inspections. Effectively, this means that the agency's commitment to flexible enforcement can be based only on past, rather than current, behavior—firms choosing minimal compliance will be able to slip through the looser monitoring associated with flexible enforcement. Similarly, the firm must decide its level of compliance prior to knowing what the next inspector from the agency will do. Both face an intractable dilemma since neither knows if the other will be tempted to make a sucker out of it.

Fortunately, the dilemma becomes more tractable if the game is repeated over and over, as is true in the regulatory arena. Then the long-term gains from voluntary compliance can provide greater rewards than do the short-term temptations to choose minimal compliance. Axelrod (1984) has demonstrated that a very simple strategy called "tit-for-tat" will ensure that an opponent will have no long-term temptation to cheat. In the regulatory context, an agency using this strategy would reward firms that have a record of flexible compliance by using flexible enforcement and punish firms that have a record of minimal compliance by using maximal enforcement. I have demonstrated elsewhere (Scholz 1984a) that under normal regulatory conditions this cooperative strategy will induce firms to choose flexible compliance as long as they are sufficiently concerned with future enforcement encounters.

By being vengeful, this cooperative strategy discourages minimal compliance. By being forgiving, it encourages firms to move from minimal to flexible compliance. As firms switch to flexible compliance, the agency can focus its limited prosecutorial resources on a decreasing number of minimal compliers. This, in turn, increases the expected penalty for the noncompliers, which in turn can increase the standard of flexible compliance acceptable to the agency. The optimal flexible compliance standard would provide the highest level of desired policy outcome for the lowest combination of compliance and monitoring-prosecutorial costs.

From agency chiefs to field inspectors, enforcement officials describe this strategy in different words: To maintain voluntary compliance, you have to hit hard at the bad apples to keep them from spoiling the good ones. Persuasion and education will work with the good firms, but only if you find and prosecute the bad ones. Educational and cooperative gestures alone do not ensure the combination of vengefulness and forgiveness of a tit-for-tat strategy. The clearest mark of the cooperative strategy is the concentration of enforcement activities on fewer firms. Cooperative strategies should therefore exhibit higher percentages of serious citations, higher percentages of penalties imposed for serious violations, larger penalties per citation, a greater number of shorter inspections with no citations (after all, you have to make sure that the cooperators are still cooperating), a high percentage of fines imposed on a small percentage of firms, and so on.

The advantages of cooperative enforcement extend beyond the enforcement process. To the extent that rules are applied flexibly and not enforced where they are impractical, the burden of creating single standards applicable across all possible circumstances will be eased.

Flexible enforcement reduces the inefficient costs associated with any given standard of performance and therefore may foster agreement to higher standards than can be achieved when legalistic enforcement is expected.

As Bardach and Kagan (1982) have argued, flexible enforcement at its best would function to improve current standards and to help anticipate problem areas not covered by current regulations before disasters occur. When enforcement agencies are focused on the social problem responsible for regulation, rather than the specific rules to be enforced, they are in the best position to see the problems and inefficiencies resulting from current regulations. An effective enforcement agency would therefore have a routine review function to amend rules and adapt them to the situation they encounter. Furthermore, an effective agency would routinely use the monitoring function of inspectors to alert them to new problems. The agency can then act as a catalyst, bringing together experts from all concerned interests to work out appropriate ways to handle new hazards before the problem becomes unmanageable (Scholz 1984c). In short, the role of strict enforcer becomes only one of several functions expected from the regulatory agency.

POLITICAL IMPEDIMENTS TO COOPERATIVE ENFORCEMENT

Even though cooperative enforcement may in theory be socially optimal, an agency's political environment may not encourage cooperative enforcement. I will discuss two major impediments that must be addressed to improve the possibilities for more desirable cooperative enforcement.

1. *Political interests do not favor cooperative enforcement.* Perhaps the biggest initial impediment is the lack of support by policy proponents and opponents. Both sides are concerned first with the specific standards being promulgated and second with the level of enforcement. The beneficiaries of regulatory policy want higher standards and higher enforcement levels, while regulated firms generally want lower standards and lower enforcement levels. The level at any given time is determined by the vagaries of political power, but the conflictive nature of the relationship remains.

Such conflict encourages enforcers to vary the stringency of enforcement in line with current power configurations, but certainly does not encourage them to pursue a truly cooperative (rather than just weak) strategy. The inevitable inefficiencies of regulation are magnified in the process. Enforcers are unable to take advantage of flexibility to increase the desired output, be it cleaner air, better health, or more safety. Furthermore, rule-making procedures must produce rules that will be applied inflexibly across many different conditions. If political interests on both sides would agree to support cooperative enforcement, on the other hand, both rule making and enforcement practices could take advantage of the greater efficiencies arising from greater flexibility. Only political education can solve this problem.

The problem is exacerbated by the incentives facing leaders of organizations that lobby for policy proponents and opponents. Although cooperation may be good for both groups as a whole, espousing cooperation is less likely to increase lobbying funds than attacking the opposition is. Again, an informed membership that appreciates the advantages of true cooperative strategies and would demand such strategies of organizational and political leaders is the primary way to minimize this problem.

2. *Cooperative enforcement is more difficult to control.* Regulatory advocates have a particularly difficult time supporting cooperative enforcement because the potential benefits in terms of efficiency have to be considered against the potential negative effects if the agency is captured by business interests, corrupted, and demoralized. Cooperative enforcement requires discretion to reward cooperative firms and punish noncooperative ones. Such discretion increases business incentives to influence and possibly corrupt the "street-level" inspectors since they would have the authority to overlook violations that would then go undetected and unpunished.

At the same time, discretion decreases the ability of the central office of oversight agencies to monitor and control the field behavior of inspectors (Scholz 1984b). It is easy to count the number of citations and inspections performed by an inspector pursuing a deterrence strategy, but much more difficult to know how much good came from the flexible enforcement trade-offs the inspector made while pursuing a cooperative strategy. Thus, concern with controlling inspectorate behavior is likely to lead to increased scrutiny of countable activities and to displacement of the real, but less measurable, goals of regulation. Again, the inspector is given little incentive to pursue the required flexible enforcement strategy.

The risks associated with cooperative enforcement were particularly salient in the polarized political environment of the 1970s that created the social regulatory agencies. The provisions for automatic penalties, limited prosecutorial discretion, and citizen enforcement initiatives written into the enforcement sections of regulatory statutes signaled a fear of agency "capture" and an attempt to ensure a stringent, noncooperative style of enforcement (Bardach and Kagan 1982).

These provisions may have arisen in part from a misunderstanding about the effectiveness of cooperative enforcement. But they primarily reflected the frustrating problem that proenforcement groups inevitably face in controlling agency discretion, particularly when the president and the administration are perceived as being probusiness.

REDUCING IMPEDIMENTS TO COOPERATIVE ENFORCEMENT

While more efficient and effective regulation and regulatory enforcement are clearly possible, improvements are unlikely unless the long-run benefits of cooperation are clear for *all* participants in the process. Otherwise, the temptation of proponents and opponents of regulation to use short-run political advantages to raise or lower standards and enforcement stringency will inevitably lead to continued confrontation and the resultant inefficiencies associated with legalistic enforcement.

The remainder of this chapter discusses several steps that could increase the likelihood of establishing a general political commitment to a less confrontational model of enforcement.

1. *Demonstrate and publicize the advantages of cooperative enforcement.* There is still little understanding of the difference between regulatory enforcement and the classical notion of enforcing criminal laws. It is important to establish convincing examples of flexible regulation that works, to rigorously evaluate the advantages and costs of ongoing programs, and to publicize the results to all groups concerned with regulation. Examples need to be developed and worked into the regulatory curriculum in schools of business, law, and public administration and in the professional schools that train the experts involved in regulatory policy decisions.

2. *Enhance the capability of existing agencies to pursue cooperative enforcement strategies.* Current model programs are useful in demonstrating innovative enforcement approaches, but have limited impact on the bulk of agency activities. To broaden the potential advantages of cooperative enforcement, two basic enhancements would be necessary. First, agencies would require greater resources to recruit, train, and retain the kind of personnel required for high-quality enforcement. Flexible enforcement requires a highly skilled inspectorate capable of making appropriate trade-offs between compliance costs and social benefits. The better trained the inspectorate, the more discretion that can be entrusted to the street level, and the greater the potential efficiency that can be gained from trade-offs.

Second, an established body of knowledge on enforcement needs to be developed through the sharing of experience across agency jurisdictions. There is surprisingly little communication between agencies despite the similarities in enforcement problems. Each agency must "reinvent the wheel" in its approach to generic problems in dealing with small or marginal businesses, for example. Each agency must rely on the common sense of experienced agents (if they are available), which may or may not be right in their opinion of effective approaches to a particular problem facing that agency. There is little systematic evaluation of the effectiveness of particular techniques and almost no sharing of such techniques across agencies (outside of special interagency task forces).

One consequence of a lack of established "enforcement technology" is that it is difficult to convince outsiders that anything but finding and punishing violations is important for enforcement. A second problem is that inspectors, supervisors, and program managers must learn about enforcement on the job. Efficient enforcement requires a better method of ensuring that enforcers are aware of the range of possible techniques that could be applied in situations as they arise. Cooperative enforcement in particular requires a more systematic knowledge about *enforcement*, not just agency rules and procedures or the substantive area of concern.

While business interests are more likely in general to support cooperative enforcement, they are also traditionally less likely to support higher budgets for enforcement agencies and for improved enforcement techniques. Yet such resources are critical to the development of a more sensible program of cooperative enforcement.

3. *Develop adequate oversight and management systems to control the discretion required for cooperative enforcement.* The greatest obstacle to cooperative enforcement is probably gaining the support of regulatory advocates. They rightfully need assurances that cooperative enforcement, in fact, would achieve greater benefits for them than the current emphasis on legalistic enforcement does. How will inspectors use their discretion? How can agency directors or oversight committees be sure that the kinds of trade-offs being made are consistent with policy guidelines? How can firms know that their competitors are not getting bigger breaks from the agency than they are?

The problem of controlling discretion is not unique to cooperative enforcement. But the need for flexibility and long-term commitments reduces the utility of normal methods based on routine reassignment of inspectors and evaluations based on counts of inspections, citations, and penalties. New systems must be developed that can earn the trust of all groups concerned with enforcement.

The development of such systems will require a conscious effort to establish suitable controls that still allow flexibility. Scholars have speculated about the nature of suitable control systems, but the current lack of knowledge has led to little agreement. Bardach and Kagan (1982) and Scholz (1984b) discuss the need for management and monitoring techniques that could reduce concerns about cooptation and capture. Ayres and Braithwaite (1989) note the difficulty with such techniques and suggest instead the need to decentralize decisions and expand the role of policy beneficiaries in enforcement. A tripartite enforcement process routinely involving business, representatives of regulatory beneficiaries, and the enforcement agency as equals at the plant level might provide all players with positive incentives to cooperate. In one model program, OSHA empowered safety committees composed of union and management representatives to enforce regulations in selected plants.

The difficulty in this system is to provide beneficiaries with incentives to cooperate in reducing regulatory inefficiencies, while controlling the temptation to take maximal advantage of enforcement opportunities, a common concern among opponents of the private attorney general notion (Sigler and Murphy 1988). Consequently, Scholz (1989) suggested that local enforcement policy should involve elected officials, rather than interest groups, arguing that electoral incentives blunt the temptation to seek maximal advantage.

WHAT CAN BE DONE

The discussion to this point paints a rather gloomy picture about the possibilities of gaining the advantages achievable through cooperative enforcement. Indeed, the kind of political education process necessary as a foundation for cooperation will require a stronger base of knowledge than is currently available. But the process has already begun with the recognition that the current level of regulatory inefficiencies is not inevitable. Agencies are experimenting with specialized programs and with more general activities to enhance compliance on a broad front.

The most useful step at this point may be to develop some institutional focus to encourage debate among *all* groups concerned with regulatory enforcement and to develop systematic knowledge relevant to that debate. By bringing together enforcement officials, business groups, and regulatory advocates from a variety of policy arenas, the critical impediments to a more cooperative approach to regulation can be explored and clarified. This can yield a set of research questions to be addressed in a series of seminars. The seminars would bring together enforcement and compliance experts from various regulatory areas, including both scholars and practitioners. The purpose would be to develop a more systematic understanding of the enforcement process in areas where general consensus exists and to suggest the most important areas for research and experimentation where less certainty exists.

The initial task of this institutional center would be to enhance the political education process necessary for the development of cooperative regulation. Future developments could focus on improving the "technologies" of regulatory enforcement and compliance and on disseminating innovative ideas across policy areas. Given the immense costs associated with regulation and regulatory enforcement, it is surprising that something like a National Academy of Regulatory Enforcement does not already exist. Such an institution could bring together creative individuals with different relevant experiences to focus on common problems of enforcement. It could expose middle and upper management in enforcement agencies, corporations, and interest groups to the range of problems and solutions developed in other regulatory arenas. Case materials developed by such discussions can be used in the business, law, and graduate schools training future leaders who will be involved in regulation. Finally, the atmosphere of such an institute may provide the isolation from political struggles in particular policy arenas necessary to allow leaders from diverse interest groups to develop a greater consensus in support of cooperative enforcement and interactive compliance.

12

Corporate Conduct in the 1990s

Jay A. Sigler and Joseph E. Murphy

MOVING FROM THE 1980s TO THE 1990s

The 1980s have been viewed by many as an anything-goes era reflecting the deregulatory approach of the Reagan administration. We have witnessed dramatic examples of corporate lawbreaking including headline-grabbing insider trading cases and savings and loan fraud.

At the beginning of the 1990s it appears that the new theme may well be "the cops are back." In reaction to the perception of unbridled misconduct there are renewed calls for re-regulation and tougher enforcement against corporate America. This raises the question, however, of whether this essentially binary approach—deregulate or re-regulate—is the only choice. Are we destined to continue a recurring pattern of free-market abuse inevitably followed by regulatory abuse?

We believe that there is a viable alternative and that it is time for an interactive or cooperative approach to corporate compliance with the law. In *Interactive Corporate Compliance* (1988), we proposed a new relationship between business and government that would rely less on litigating and more on encouraging self-regulatory efforts by business. For those corporations willing to work in this manner, government would assist and encourage their development of effective compliance programs. Judged by the experiences and practices described by the contributors to this book and by our discussions with others, we believe that this concept is fairly well understood and that there are substantial opportunities for moving in this direction.

The interactive model, however, goes beyond the relationship of government and business and also addresses interaction within the corporation. This point appears to be not as well understood by those who work outside of the corporate environment. There is still a tendency to view corporations in a simplified way as if they were individuals making rational cost-benefit analyses in order to decide whether they should comply with the law. We see interactive compliance within the corporation as requiring management to make compliance and business ethics part of the management process. The compliance program would be integrated into management's system of incentives and controls; the operation of an effective management system then involves interaction with all of the complex forces within the corporation.

This internal interactive process also occurs on the group and departmental levels within the organization, empowering and relying on those groups that naturally tend to support compliance efforts. To understand this concept, it is necessary to recognize pluralistic elements within corporations. Modern corporations are not merely monolithic structures that take on the personality or characteristics of discrete humans. Rather, they are complex organizations affected by interaction among constituent groups within the institution. In *Interactive Corporate Compliance* (1988), Sigler and I identified certain groups, designated as "compliance constituencies," that, by their nature, tend to support compliance objectives. Interactive compliance theory is constructed on the basis of identifying those actors within corporations who have an institutional or professional interest in supporting the requirements of regulatory bodies and who have loyalties beyond the boundaries of their employment. For example, corporate legal departments, auditors, and safety engineers have external standards that place limits on their allegiance to corporate objectives. If these constituencies are appropriately empowered within the corporation, they may act as a strong force to inhibit lawbreaking and to assure positive conduct.

Both elements of interaction (i.e., between government and business, and within the corporation) are necessary to have effective compliance programs. Government involvement should be used to enhance the role of the compliance constituencies, and effective compliance constituencies will help to ensure the government's compliance objectives.

WHAT ARE THE ALTERNATIVES TO INTERACTIVE COMPLIANCE?

As society addresses the question of business misconduct, what are the choices it faces? Perhaps the most politically appealing is the hypercriminalization of business conduct. Criminalizing business conduct is an area where the United States leads the global community. It is probably safe to assume that this country has more criminal legislation on its books relating to corporate conduct and engages in more criminal enforcement activity against corporations than do any of its major trading partners. It should not be surprising therefore that the current reaction to the 1980s includes increasing numbers of proposals to further criminalize corporate conduct.

In *Corporate Crime and Violence* (1988), Russell Mokhiber provides one of the starkest examples of this faith in the criminal law system. His work is a provocative catalog of corporate wrongdoing. In addition to his encyclopedic coverage of business misconduct, Mokhiber proposes a "50-point law-and-order program to curb corporate crime" (1988, 38–65). His proposals include adding citizen-bounty provisions to federal laws and "executing" corporations in serious cases. It is evidently Mokhiber's view that only fear of punishment will keep corporate managers from despoiling society and that more laws and more lawyers are the only solution. In this he follows the lead of well-known reformer Ralph Nader, who has exhibited the same antibusiness attitudes.

While Mokhiber's approach reflects a well-defined antibusiness perspective, the views of the United States Sentencing Commission (1989), although more moderate in tone, also evolved from this same assumption that increased criminal sanctions against corporations are necessary if society is to control corporate crime. The proposals offered by this commission in 1989 included potential fines of over $300 million and the prospect of judicial management through probation for certain corporate offenders. While the commission's proposals did recognize a role for voluntary corporate compliance by offering a potential 20 percent sentence reduction, this mitigating feature is not significant enough to detract from the overwhelmingly punitive approach of the guidelines.

The criminalization approach has been taken even so far that one court attempted to impose "incarceration" on an entire corporation. In *United States v. Allegheny Bottling Co.*, 695 F. Supp. 856 (E.D. Va. 1988), a court faced with antitrust violations by a corporation concluded it could imprison the company by seizing its assets. It then suspended the sentence and imposed community service obligations as a condition to probation. Although this effort was rejected by an appellate court, it stands as an example of the view that a greater degree of punishment and greater resources are needed to enhance society's ability to correct corporate wrongdoing. If enforcers can only discover a punishment so total and terrifying that business managers will be shocked into compliance, then the problem will be solved—or so the theory appears to go.

A second cousin of hypercriminalization is the notion that corporate conduct can be reformed by inviting more litigation against corporations. Under this banner, additional legislation is proposed to create new causes of action for business misconduct, and bounties are offered to private parties for the pursuit of such wrongdoers as inside traders and fraudulent government contractors. As history has shown, the likely result is additional costs imposed on society by the litigation system and the potential for misdirecting corporate conduct to avoid any form of risk, even for otherwise legitimate activities, because of the prohibitive exposure of civil litigation (Huber 1988). Private litigation as a supplement to prosecution may be a deterrent to antisocial business behavior, but it comes at a high cost of litigation abuse and wasteful corporate defense activities.

A somewhat more moderate approach is championed by those who propose inserting representatives of other societal interests into the corporation. Ralph Nader and his colleagues, in *Taming the Giant Corporation* (1976), have proposed placing representatives who will reflect external interests on corporations' boards of directors. Ian Ayres and John Braithwaite, in their ground-breaking work on the theory of tripartism (1989), suggest that public interest groups be introduced into relations between business and government in order to provide this type of balance. We think that some moderate role for public interest groups could be useful at times and deserves further exploration, but we reserve judgment on any effort to force this approach on businesses.

The societal intrusion approach reaches its most coercive level in the probation concept, as proposed in the U.S. Sentencing Commission Guidelines. This approach, which is strongly supported by Professor John C. Coffee, Jr., (1990), would have a representative of the government taking over a management role in corporations. Thus, a recidivistic corporation that had previously failed to follow requirements of the law would be deprived of the opportunity to commit future violations by having government management substituted for private management.

This, at least, is a more direct approach than reliance on criminal and civil litigation. It attempts to address directly the source of corporate wrongdoing and to intercede before such wrongdoing can occur. On its face, preemptive intervention or intrusion would certainly strike an observer as being more logical than relying on mere threats of litigation. In military terms, for example, a strong army may be an excellent deterrent, but no defense is as sure as completely occupying an enemy's capital. On a short-term basis this takes away an opponent's ability to cause harm.

There are very serious risks, however, in taking this approach. Its proponents tend to downplay the almost violently negative reaction it draws from corporations. One should not lightly suggest to a corporate manager that someone in government or the consumer movement should be added to his or her management team or even replace that team altogether. While a manager may understand why he or she must face a prison term or expensive litigation for violating the laws, there is likely to be no sympathy for or cooperation with such forced intrusion prior to a violation.

Even in the case where a violation is a condition precedent for the intrusion, as would be the case for probation, this approach comes with potentially high costs and substantial disruption. While one must by sympathetic to society's need to prevent violations, one must also not forget that corporations are generally highly efficient engines of modern economies. Inserting consumer representatives or government probation officers into the economic system will inevitably disrupt business organizations and add substantially to the cost of their operation. How could a court-appointed probation officer effectively manage a microchip manufacturer or a multinational services provider? How could a corporation deal with fast-moving foreign competitors when its decisions require the concurrence of consumer, environmental, and labor representatives? How many probation officers or public interest spokespersons will know how to manage a sales force or understand corporate strategic planning?

As a result of these conflicts it is likely that the corporate body will isolate and effectively cut off any such intruders. While the probation officer or the public interest board member may think he or she is in charge, he or she may well find that the corporation has developed informal systems that will bypass this interference. In fact, less rather than more of the crucially important information necessary to monitor compliance efforts will be brought to the top of the organization in order to circumvent this perceived intrusion.

There is also a grave concern that such artificial interference will result in forced compliance efforts that will fail miserably. Court-ordered probation officers and public interest advocates will probably sponsor compliance programs that will be poorly conceived and implemented because of the advocate's lack of knowledge and experience. Experience with government-imposed compliance programs shows a history of formalistic and ineffective efforts, demonstrating little understanding of corporate dynamics or effective management. The result may even be harmful to the proponents of voluntary interactive compliance techniques that could otherwise be effective. Ultimately, then, we must disagree with the approach of the U.S.

Sentencing Commission and find it at variance with organizational experience. Instead, we believe that legal recognition and endorsement of self-enforcement practices will prove much more effective than reliance on direct public intervention. While use of some punitive measures will always be necessary, increasing the role of voluntary compliance is the key to interactive compliance.

Some of those who recognize the value of voluntary compliance have also developed the idea that it may be possible to compel corporations to undertake self-enforcement programs. This approach does not go so far as that which would insert outsiders into the inner workings of the corporation. Its proponents recognize that corporations themselves are the entities best placed to ensure legal and ethical conduct. Thus, John Braithwaite, in his insightful work on enforced self-regulation (1982), notes the ability of corporations to engage in self-policing, but laments the absence of motivation to do so. He suggests that government's role may be to require such internal efforts. Similarly, the U.S. Defense Department in dealing with improper conduct by government contractors has flirted with the idea of requiring compliance programs.

The proponents of this idea are correct in their assessment of corporate internal policing activities, but it is unlikely that compelling "voluntary" compliance would be an effective method. As long as compliance activities are alien and compelled from outside, they will naturally be resisted by the corporate organization. Rather than being interactive, the approach is likely to be antagonistic. Moreover, this has the same weakness as other compulsory programs in that it is inherently closed-ended. That is, any time a program is compulsory the participants will have an incentive to minimize the impact. This will invite a form of gamesmanship in which the corporation seeks to comply with the legal requirements by doing nothing more than the minimum. Such approaches tend to stifle innovation and limit the effectiveness and flexibility of the programs.

While the 1990s are witnessing renewed interest in additional criminalization of business conduct and proposals for outside intrusion into corporations, a very different school of thought is represented by some proponents of business ethics who are inclined to rely on rhetoric and appeals to managers' higher ideals and principles. They do not believe in relying on government merely to enforce the law because society needs more than this. What they call for is managers who take the public interest into account and who are taught in business school to consider ethical and societal interests in their decision making. Advocates of this view promote the notion that corporations can "do well by doing good." If only more business schools and more corporations would open themselves up to this enlightened message, the ethical (and presumably legal) performance of business would improve.

We are sympathetic to the points that underlie this approach. In the long term for business to be successful it must be attuned to society's needs. Business managers who are driven only by shallow economic analyses are likely to lead their institutions into a collision course with society. But we are deeply skeptical that the rhetoric of business ethics can compete with the real-world demands of the marketplace and the daily pressures of peer groups. It is difficult to convince people that ethical conduct is desirable in the long run when in the short run the thieves drive Cadillacs and Porsches. While students might leave a business ethics class with an academic understanding of the professor's sense of values, if there is no further reinforcement of these views, the work place will eventually erode the impact of those messages. Instead, what is needed is a system that reinforces those values on a day-to-day basis. Inculcation of ethical values in business dealings is valuable, but insufficient to attain corporate responsiveness to society's goals and policies.

WHY GOVERNMENT WILL LOSE THE WAR ON CORPORATE CRIME

In efforts to control corporate conduct we see a need both for strong enforcement of criminal law against deliberate wrongdoers and for effective measures to remind business students and business managers of the need to respect society's values. While we do not think that the rhetoric of business ethics will be effective on the latter point, we also do not think that the increased emphasis on criminal enforcement will be more effective in controlling corporate conduct. In the past, criminalization has neither eliminated improper conduct nor resulted in business institutions in which business ethics or society's values have taken on increased stature. We believe that a massive campaign against corporate wrongdoing that draws unthinkingly on past precedents and does not grapple with the real world of large business organizations is destined to fail. Worse than this, it may impair the efficiency of business without any incremental benefit to society.

As a beginning point it is fundamentally ironic that proponents of increased criminalization for corporations point with indignation at a perceived disparity between the treatment of individuals and the treatment of corporations for the commission of crimes (Mokhiber 1988). The logic of this argument should be premised on the idea that if a method has worked in one environment, it should then be applied to the other. Putting aside for the moment the issue of whether corporations should be analogized to individuals, there is a threshold question of whether criminalization has, in fact, been effective in dealing with individual conduct. This is certainly a subject which is open to endless debate and in which one will search in vain for consensus. For example, no one has yet demonstrated that the reintroduction of capital punishment has decreased the number of capital offenses in the United States. Nor has it been shown that increased criminal enforcement alone will resolve the drug problem. For every voice that insists on increased criminal enforcement there is another voice that speaks of the need for societal reform, educational programs, and economic intervention. Criminologists are not agreed that increases in penalties result in deterrence among potential criminals. If it is not clear that criminalization has worked successfully in dealing with individual crimes, where it is relatively easy to apply, then it does not logically follow that increased criminalization is a panacea for corporate misconduct.

If one looks at the track record in applying criminal law to business conduct, it is also difficult to make the case that more criminalization is needed. The United States, at the state and federal levels, has shown no reluctance to criminalize business conduct. The list of areas is seemingly endless: antitrust, the environment, drug safety, government contracting, technology exports, and so on. Yet it is difficult to point with satisfaction to the results of this process. Even in the areas in which misconduct has been criminal for decades there are still continuing patterns of violations. Moreover, as quickly as a new area is criminalized, yet another area of misconduct develops to be met by new criminal penalties. Perhaps the proponents of criminalization should take the time to read the daily reports of business crime on the front page of the *Wall Street Journal* before they make their assessment of the effectiveness of these programs. As long as our system prompts business managers to compete with government in a contest to circumvent the law, history leaves little doubt that society will always lose that contest.

Even if the track record of criminalization were more impressive in terms of preventing business misconduct, however, it has long been recognized that there are profound flaws in applying the criminal justice system to modern corporations. In the words of one commentator, there is "no soul to damn, no body to kick" (King 1977, 1). How does one effectively punish and deter an institution with 50,000 employees and 5,000 managers spread around the world, a board of directors that meets only for a few hours four times a year, and hundreds of thousands of stockholders who have no significant contact with the corporation and who may own the stock for only a few months or a few days at a time?

Those who propose criminal punishment work from the model that some evil group is making a calculated economic decision to sacrifice the public good for private benefit. It is likely that those commentators who operate from this model have never, in fact, experienced corporate decision making. While individuals concerned with their own personal well-being may make decisions using this model, institutions generally do not. Rather, decisionmaking tends to be diffused in a group context. Time and again the same pattern recurs. At the highest levels of the corporation generalized directions are given for corporate conduct. The board or CEO will exhort all managers to increase revenue. Managers further down the chain interpret these directions based on a variety of inputs. Somewhere near the bottom of the chain, managers make specific decisions that may run afoul of the law, but believe that more senior managers have supported this conduct. Attempting to impose penalties at any one point along the chain yields a very unsatisfying result. While one may chastise the senior managers for not being specific or thoughtful enough in their direction, it is usually very difficult to find specific intent to violate the law. At the lower levels one can identify individuals who clearly broke the law, but in most cases these individuals received little or no direct benefit from the violation. Enforcement officials sense that these small fish should not be the real targets, but they cannot find big fish with specific intent.

Faced with this diffusion of decision making, corporate enforcers then attempt to impose no-fault criminal liability for all those involved. This does not change the fact that no one individual in this chain has the moral culpability usually associated with individual criminal offenses. No-fault liability will, moreover, tend to push the corporation to avoid any innovative development of goods and services because no manager can afford to accept absolute criminal liability. Better to be less efficient or less innovative and to follow only tried and true methods than to take a personal criminal risk.

There is certainly a place for strong and relentless enforcement against those corporate officials who meet the traditional standards of culpability. A deliberate decision to dump hazardous materials or to defraud innocent consumers deserves swift punishment. Perhaps if the courts were not clogged with the results of reformers' experiments with criminalization, those types of cases would be more effective at reaching the truly bad actors. Certainly the business community would not oppose this use of the criminal law. But, instead, battles over arcane issues of discovery and interpretation of hastily drawn business criminal laws cause the system to fail even in its most basic and legitimate function: visible punishment of individuals who deliberately harm society.

When government loses its focus on individual wrongdoing and attempts to punish large corporations, the imposition of penalties on the corporation often brings unintended and dysfunctional results. Instead of reaching a few individual managers in the corporation who are responsible for a willful violation, this system tends to injure thousands or in some cases millions of innocent victims. The imposition of substantial fines and the public shaming of a corporation may cause tens of thousands of employees to suffer for the misconduct of a handful. Financial penalties that are intended to hit the shareholders result in punishment to individual investors who probably had not the slightest knowledge of the corporate violation. Considering the frequent turnover in stock ownership, in fact, those share owners who have the stock at the time of the violation have long since sold it to others. Moreover, the shareholders of large corporations tend to include individual investors and such institutions as pension funds. To the extent that the criminal action affects the value of this investment, society exacts its revenge on middle-class families attempting to save money for their children's education or their parents' retirement. If criminal punishment is truly effective and hurts the corporation, then it also necessarily hurts the corporation's customers and its suppliers. If fines in the hundreds of millions of dollars are imposed, the company's purchases of supplies and provision of products and services are likely to be disrupted or impaired. And, finally, when all of these participants are damaged, then the communities that rely on their business are also damaged. Thus, while society may initially take great satisfaction in imposing eight-or nine-figure penalties on corporate offenders, a realistic economic analysis of the result is extremely unsettling.

It may be argued, however, that society must impose severe penalties because it cannot afford the impact of corporate violations. One defective nuclear power plant, one dangerous drug, or one massive oil spill is more than society should have to bear. We fully endorse that concern, but believe that corporate punishment is often ineffective in preventing misconduct. Punishment is always by nature reactive and not preventive. It is only after the offense (and usually long after the offense) that the punishment takes effect. Only after miles of beaches are environmentally damaged do businesses get the message that this misconduct is economically unsound and will result in expensive government intervention. Even then it is a lesson whose impact is usually short-lived. In a few years many of the preventive measures hastily devised in reaction to a highly publicized prosecution tend to wither away as attention focuses on new areas of prosecution. Today's pollution control system may become a lower priority as memories of Exxon Valdez fade away and the prosecutors train their litigation guns on other targets.

It is exactly the magnitude of these risks that requires more than reactive criminal controls. This need calls for an active and effective system of intervention in corporations that will deter such misconduct. Environmental cleanup for the truly unavoidable accident, for example, is cheaper and more effective when corporations take steps in advance to anticipate environmental risks. Society needs to find ways to encourage industry to use its most innovative and ambitious engineers and managers to develop methods to minimize such risks. There is a need for fewer lawyers working on innovative legal theories for punishing environmental harm after the fact and more managers working on avoiding that harm before it happens.

The war on corporate crime also will fail as a deterrent. Criminalization relies solely on fear as a motivator. However, every important segment of our society relies on positive incentives and not just negatives to achieve results. It is not simply fear of punishment that drives our major institutions—corporations, governments, universities—to achieve results.

For purposes of controlling corporate conduct, fear certainly has a role to play. It may be a necessary element, but it is clearly not sufficient. As they taught in high school biology, the reaction to fear is either "flight" or "fight." Those with the "flight" reaction may make efforts to increase compliance. On the other hand, they may respond with a "head in the sand" reaction. Those whose reaction to fear is "fight" may simply go underground in their misconduct and decide to show the government who is stronger. Moreover, fear tends to be a short-term factor. And fear of a remote risk may be overcome by fear of an immediate risk. Thus, the new manager who is afraid that some day he may be punished may have his willpower overcome by the immediate risk that he will be fired or demoted if he does not respond to his supervisor's improper demands. The fear generated by corporate managers and peer groups is an immediate fear; the fear generated by the potential wrath of society is always more distant.

On an institutional basis, criminalization and the use of fear result in a closed-ended and not expansive reaction. In order to avoid penalties an economically driven corporation will engage in only the minimum amount of compliance necessary to avoid prosecution. The corporation will do exactly what is required and will not take chances with additional efforts. Thus, criminalization does not encourage experimentation in compliance to develop more effective techniques. Nor does it utilize those competitive forces that otherwise are the drivers of the American economy. An interactive compliance program would have corporations competing to develop the most effective compliance methods. As long as criminalization is the model, however, the whole thrust is at odds with the competitive urge. In a criminal litigation system the most effective competitor would be the one that achieves the minimum compliance utilizing the minimum resources and that exploits every means to avoid the impact of the law. This results in nominal compliance systems that repeatedly fail to deter corporate misconduct.

Hypercriminalization also tends to distort corporate behavior in unpredictable and socially dysfunctional ways. If an area is perceived to be too risky, the larger and more economically sound corporations will avoid the area entirely. The risky function will then be left either to foreign enterprises or to businesses willing to accept the risk of criminal and financial punishment. In an overdeterrence system it is inevitable that not only socially improper conduct, but also other conduct that would benefit society, would be deterred.

DEVELOPMENT OF INTERACTIVE CORPORATE COMPLIANCE

The fundamentals of interactive corporate compliance and its background are set forth in Chapter 1. We deal here with the elements needed to develop this approach and move it forward. Interactive compliance seeks to draw from three institutions: government, business, and universities.

In government there is a need for change in all three branches. The judiciary needs to accept the value of less litigation-oriented approaches. It must see that not only is concern for protecting and encouraging corporate compliance a device for avoiding the rigors of litigation battles, but also it represents a socially beneficial objective that may weigh more heavily in the balance than the more remote benefits derived from the litigation system. The executive branch needs to work with business in promoting compliance efforts. It must see its objective as enhancing compliance, not just prosecuting lawsuits. And the legislature needs to enact programs with a more interactive approach. Lawmakers need to support and enable experiments in cooperative enforcement so the participants may learn what works and build on those successes.

In the category of business we include internal management as well as those who provide professional services to these institutions. Participants in the business arena must open their minds to the possibility of working with government and accept the need for innovative techniques in compliance programs. They must hold compliance programs to the same standards that are used to measure other management programs: Do the programs work? Do they cause employees to understand and follow the law? Or are they just rehashes of old legal lectures that the audiences ignore?

In the universities there must be changes in the educational approaches of business and law schools. Business managers (and even future business lawyers) need training in how to manage for compliance results and how to work cooperatively with the government. Law students need to be taught that there is more to be done than litigation in the legal system and that compliance is an important element of their practice. Concepts of legal ethics and professionalism need to be reexamined to see if they effectively maximize corporate counsel's role and responsibility in preventing corporate wrongdoing. Universities need to be encouraged to contribute research and analysis to the development of cooperative compliance efforts and of a more useful understanding of corporate organizational dynamics.

In our work since the publication of *Interactive Corporate Compliance* (1988), we have discerned three relatively distinct schools of thought on corporate conduct: (1) corporate compliance, (2) business ethics, and (3) law enforcement and public policy.

The corporate compliance community consists primarily of lawyers and those closely aligned with corporate legal staffs. They tend to be legalistic in approach and to be caught up primarily by precedents. That is, there is a tendency to use only those compliance devices that have been used by others. There tends not to be an emphasis on measurable results unless such measurements are required by government (e.g., in EEO programs). Those who participate in this effort tend to be very sincere in their desire to assure compliance with the law. They also tend, however, not to identify with the moral language of the business ethicist, although they are equally sincere in their devotion.

The second group is those who are involved in the business ethics movement. They tend to focus primarily on individual decision making and value analysis. There is great devotion to following the values of society, but too often there is an absence of practical orientation in this program. They also tend to understate the role of groups and institutional dynamics in their focus on individual decision making. Their message may be an important one, but its impact is far too transitory.

The business ethicists are correct, however, to go beyond the requirements of the law and to look beyond precedents. Those who understand this point in the corporate compliance environment also advise their clients that they need be concerned not only with what the law currently requires, but also with how the law will probably be expanded if businesses attempt to exploit loopholes. The business ethics effort has also developed some activists who focus on practical efforts to inculcate ethics. In these activities the business ethicists come closest to the corporate compliance community.

The third group focuses on enforcement and policy analysis. Too many in this school tend to be hindered by their dedication to criminal enforcement and avoid further analysis or attention to the results. The members of the old guard in this field are content to push for increased penalties or new punitive measures and to avoid the intellectual rigors of questioning their underlying assumptions. There are, however, those in public policy like Louis S. Bezich who are concerned with finding techniques that will work in the attempt to understand and change the dynamics of corporate conduct.

Those in the old guard of this community are right in their assessment that willful misconduct must be punished. But they have much to learn from their colleagues who are willing to try a mix of negative and positive techniques to achieve the desired result.

We are attempting in our work to create a common effort among these three schools of thought. This is extraordinarily difficult because each group uses its own language and consists of very different practitioners. We have emphasized, however, that they all have a single focus: corporate conduct. Each needs to develop more of a results orientation, rather than working from old and unchallenged premises. Each needs to develop more pragmatic and enduring approaches. And each needs to consider a more positive role for the government in this process.

THE CONTRIBUTORS: WHAT IS TO BE DONE

The contributors to *Corporate Lawbreaking and Interactive Compliance* represent the three institutions we seek to address: government, business, and universities.

These chapters were prepared by some of the most knowledgeable people in their fields who are concerned with specific measures to improve the regulatory atmosphere that has dominated business-government relations. Each contributor has had some direct personal experience in the field or in teaching, and each attempts to provide a new approach to government-business interaction. The results are a fresh look at the subject and a host of new ideas and experiments which are gathered here for the first time. Recognition of the need to bring together the proponents of these new ideas was the driving force behind this work and a related April 21, 1990, conference at

New York University's Leonard Stern School of Business. The conference, held under the auspices of the Samuel and May Rudin Foundation, the Stern School, and the Business Ethics Study Team, Inc., brought together many of the contributors, as well as other commentators, to share their experiences and to debate each other.

The common theme was the prevention of corporate lawbreaking. The common feeling was that traditional strict enforcement by criminal and civil litigation was not sufficient. Injunctions to adopt ethical codes were insufficient. Traditional business and legal education was not serving the needs of the society or of the students. The result of these concerns was this volume of valuable contributions to the development of interactive compliance. The authors' analyses and suggestions help give specific content and direction to this effort.

Interactive Compliance in Government

The chapter by New York State Attorney General Robert Abrams shows a growing convergence between enlightened enforcement policy guided by a tough, but effective, prosecutor and the more cooperative approaches advocated in *Interactive Corporate Compliance* (Sigler and Murphy 1988). While he does not endorse all of the Sigler-Murphy approach, Abrams realizes that American corporations have come a long way in meeting their social and ethical responsibilities and are capable of correcting their conduct toward social ends. Yet, as a rigorous, enforcement-minded prosecutor, Abrams has waged many battles against industrial polluters and other corporate backsliders and criminals. He has few illusions about the ethical or legal standards followed by some American corporations.

Nonetheless, Abrams recognizes the need for greater public-private cooperation because of the magnitude of the task of enforcing environmental regulations. In this field in particular he suggests a new strategy of preventive enforcement, which anticipates environmental damage and depends on industry to develop techniques to avoid pollution incidents through internal corporate control measures. Readers can appreciate the fresh approach that Abrams offers, although his specific proposal of reliance on environmental audits seems to us to be limited and lacking in sufficient incentives for industry cooperation. Still, it is impressive to see an official whose task is to pursue wrongdoers concerned with a larger vision of protecting the environment through greater cooperation between business and government.

Indeed, Abrams may have a more pragmatic sense of what is politically possible than the Sigler-Murphy approach allows. The bill that Abrams prepared for the New York State legislature is designed to reduce the risk of the release of hazardous substances by requiring all facilities that deal with extremely hazardous materials to prepare a risk management plan. This risk management plan would be prepared for the state commissioner of environmental conservation who would review each plan quarterly for compliance. In essence, the bill mandates a self-enforcement plan and an emergency response plan for each such facility. However, each plan would be developed by the company itself, according to its own internal control plan. While mandatory in tone, the bill does rest on planning for a form of self-regulation. In seeking to avoid a Bhopal, India, tragedy in this nation, New York State would require higher standards of accident prevention techniques than current law requires.

Interactive Corporate Compliance devoted extensive discussion to the new roles for government, business, and academia in a cooperative arrangement. Missing from this analysis was consideration of a primary moving force in modern American society: the public interest group. These groups were mentioned only briefly as potential adverse litigants and were not included as factors in the corporate model described. Attorney General Abrams has helped bridge that gap by his third enforcement strategy: having citizens—and, by logical extension, their organized interest groups—reward desired business conduct with their patronage or their endorsement.

Abrams' contribution is potentially one of the most significant in the development of interactive compliance. Organized consumer support could be a potent incentive behind government programs that encourage and reward voluntary corporate compliance efforts. OSHA's Star Program and Louis S. Bezich's Silver Platter Award could take on even greater dimensions if successful participants were assured of consumer support and recognition. Moreover, it would help replace the usually acrimonious relationship between business and consumer advocate groups by providing an opportunity for constructive exchanges. Consumer watchdogs would still need to be vigilant, but they could concentrate their efforts on those businesses that reject cooperative compliance.

Corporate self-regulation through the development of effective corporate codes of conduct is discouraged in the current legal environment. That is the point that Harvey L. Pitt and Karl A. Groskaufmanis vividly prove in their erudite survey of the legal status of such codes. A much lengthier exposition of their findings was presented in the April 1990 issue of the *Georgetown Law Journal*. Those who need a detailed legal analysis of the many statutes, judicial decisions, and administrative rulings of the past two decades will want to examine that article.

For our purposes the significance of corporate codes lies largely in their failure to be used effectively in compliance efforts and their failure to generate basic changes in corporate behavior. Even though most major American corporations have adopted some version of a code of conduct, Pitt and Groskaufmanis insist that compliance programs are still inadequate. Their conclusions rest on extensive empirical surveys made over several years, although the same conclusion can be drawn from the continuing numbers of corporate convictions for violations of law. These surveys suggest very strongly that corporations have not attached sufficient penalties to code violations and may have mistakenly assumed that merely issuing a corporate conduct code was the same as having a genuine compliance program. This is an important insight for advocates of interactive corporate compliance because it suggests that corporations are not sufficiently concerned with serious infractions to police their own employees. This is not a surprising discovery. It merely demonstrates anew the failure to study the effectiveness of compliance methods, and the minimalist approach to compliance that is currently invited by the American legal system.

If the corporate code is the highest expression of the standards and expectations of the modern American corporation, then it is disquieting to view the inadequacies of these codes as revealed by this chapter. The outlook for better codes is not bleak, and the authors have suggestions for major improvements in those codes. However, there is a long distance yet to travel in the journey toward self-enforcement of responsible and legal corporate conduct.

Pitt and Groskaufmanis have worked with many corporate conduct codes. Consequently, their proposal for a new legal standard to encourage corporations to take codes more seriously is based on their legal analysis and their sense of the future of the underlying social policies involved. Because it provides for the recognition of bona fide programs, this proposal fits well within the model of interactive compliance. However, the proposal would be enhanced by a stronger and more positive certification and reward system which could help avoid the deficiencies inherent in judicial assessments of corporate compliance management. Caution is needed also in assuring that attention is given to all of the elements needed for effective compliance systems, beyond the more visible and legalistic devices such as written codes.

Pitt and Groskaufmanis do give a series of steps—a virtual checklist—for the preparation of corporate codes which can reassure judges and the general public. Companies that are contemplating revisions to their codes should consider their proposals. So should enlightened judges and prosecutors.

Jay A. Sigler's chapter builds on his earlier writing in interactive compliance by showing examples of this new approach that are already in place. There are federal and local examples, but apparently very few of them to study. Sigler suggests that each of them, while worthy in some fashion, does not exemplify a consistent approach to gaining compliance and greater cooperation between business and government for the enhancement of the policy goals that underlie the pertinent regulations. In a sense each example is a discrete experiment, lacking in reference and in theoretical design. As a result, it is surprising that these programs work as well as they do.

What is needed is a much more systematic approach to compliance, even if that approach is not grounded in the theory of interactive compliance. There must be a much more conscious effort to get corporations to do what the public and the regulators want them to do. More coercion and threats of punishment will have limited effect. Some cooperative model needs to be examined by leaders in government and business. There appear to be too few Lou Beziches in government or business.

Louis S. Bezich describes the most detailed pilot program in interactive compliance available in the nation. As administrator of Camden County, New Jersey, Bezich has spearheaded the effort to put into place most of the principles of interactive compliance. The voluntary Silver Platter program is a small effort in the area of restaurant inspection, but its development is an encouraging model of what might be done in many other communities around the country to encourage greater cooperation between business and government to the benefit of the general public.

The Camden County program does not compromise or lower standards in any way. It fully meets the legal expectations of the state of New Jersey; yet it also exceeds them by setting still higher standards of sanitation. These higher standards have been accepted by leading restaurants because of the incentive provided by the county, which amounts to a commercially valuable recognition of exceptionally high standards.

The incentives for the government are cost savings and increased compliance. The incentives for business are reputational rewards and possible advantages in reducing legal liability in suits resulting from food-borne illnesses. Some of the more progressive companies were already adhering to high standards of sanitation and were appreciative of governmental endorsement.

The elaborate story of the selling of the concept to business and government itself is well told by Bezich. This chapter reveals many of the possible points of resistance and cooperation in particular program areas. Bezich conducted the kind of analysis that will be essential in future efforts in interactive compliance.

Bezich also makes another important point that deserves emphasis. Innovation at the county and local levels is much easier and less risky than are wholesale federal programs. The experimentation possible at lower levels of government has always been a source of strength of our political system. Perhaps interactive compliance experiments conducted by state, county, and local governments are the wave of the future in business-government relations. Certainly the flexibility and knowledge gained by such experiments are worth several volumes of theory.

The Camden County Silver Platter program has just been launched and has been thoughtfully constructed to meet the objectives of interactive compliance. If it works well, similar programs can be expected in New Jersey and elsewhere in the nation. This could be the launching pad for interactive compliance in larger and more complex policy areas. The timidity of regulators and the skepticism of corporate leaders will not be easily overcome. Proofs derived from working examples are the best evidence that interactive compliance is effective. We look forward to seeing the results of the Camden County experiment, but believe that Bezich presents enough information to encourage other progressive officials to move forward in this direction right now.

Interactive Compliance in Business

Practical examples of the development and implementation of corporate self-governance programs are provided by Paul M. Carren and Richard B. Pazornik, senior executives with the government contractor advisory services unit of KPMG Peat Marwick, the internationally known public accounting firm. Government contractors are under special obligations to ensure that their performance is in compliance with laws and regulations because they are financed with public funds. Carren and Pazornik have assisted government contractors in meeting their legal obligations. Although the authors cannot reveal the names of their clients, the examples found in their chapter are based on their direct experiences with government contractors and other firms. The importance of corporate codes of conduct is underscored, and emphasis is placed on implementation issues.

Perhaps because the Carren-Pazornik approach is drawn from their experience in government contracting, it raises questions that may be very controversial in other areas of compliance. They recommend voluntary disclosure of violations, even without any commitment from government to reward companies for such salutary conduct. Yet in the current litigation context there is a high risk that this will be exploited by prosecutors and private plaintiffs. Their emphasis on documentation, such as specifying the impact of violations, may be effective in an interactive compliance system, but it could court disaster in the hands of private adverse litigants. In today's environment such steps require a great deal of guidance from experienced legal counsel.

Also controversial is the suggestion that penalties be specified for each category of violation. This would add a useful level of specificity to the compliance program, but at a cost of decreased flexibility. Moreover, in areas other than government contracting it may be impossible to quantify in advance the degree of penalty appropriate for each type of violation. Ultimately the schedule of penalties will probably be used against the company in litigation if the decreased penalties suggested for "lesser" offenses appear in hindsight to have given tacit approval to such violations.

Carren and Pazornik's suggestion to use outside, independent parties, such as independent auditing firms, to review in-house compliance programs is a valuable one, worth incorporating in an interactive program. It may add both a useful source of new insights and ideas for such programs and an additional check to assure government that the program is conducted in good faith. Again, however, in the absence of an interactive arrangement with government, this approach has substantial drawbacks. If a company relies on the attorney-client or self-evaluative privilege, introduction of third parties who are not lawyers may increase the risk of waiving the privilege. Second, use of outside professionals increases the cost of the program, particularly if the program is an ongoing one that is integrated into the day-to-day management system of the company. Also, while the use of outside auditors or accountants may be effective in reviews of financial control systems, it may raise difficult questions over legal interpretations in more qualitative areas such as antitrust and consumer protection. Nevertheless, the idea should be seriously considered, and the views of these authors should be given substantial weight in illustrating the potential value of voluntary self-governance programs.

What Bezich offers for government administrators, Joseph E. Murphy offers for their counterparts in corporate law departments. Murphy provides a detailed script for implementing interactive compliance within the corporation, drawing on his professional experience and that of other practitioners. This chapter is addressed to corporate counsel as a compliance-oriented group, but the same message could apply to any manager devoted to compliance.

Behind this chapter is more than just a "how to" lesson. It is intended to challenge corporate counsel to question the assumptions they have traditionally made. It reminds them that the compliance job is not exclusively the task of lawyers. Other skills are needed, and they must enlist the active support of nonlawyers. Outside the corporation, government must provide substantial support for the voluntary efforts of compliance constituencies within the corporation. Corporate counsel can be the catalysts for this process.

Murphy's chapter should also be seen as an invitation to government lawyers to look more realistically at the tools for corporate compliance, if companies have the incentives to use them. Interactive compliance is premised on the belief that companies can do a better job of policing themselves if they are given inducements and incentives to do so. The fifteen points discussed by Murphy, as well as the Kaplan and Pitt-Groskaufmanis chapters, give a preview of what can be done to build better voluntary compliance programs.

Jeffrey M. Kaplan's chapter represents another technique in interactive compliance. Kaplan has developed the idea of providing corporate executives and business students with terrifying examples of the consequences of wrongdoing. These examples are derived from the lives of corporate criminals who give testimony to their harrowing experiences. Convicted white collar criminals teach lessons that no textbook can convey. These lessons should become engraved on the consciousness of businesspersons so that they absorb the possible moral and legal consequences of their activities.

As Kaplan sees it, this "scared straight" program requires greater government cooperation if it is to reach the intended audiences and have the intended deterrent effect. Prosecutors must give more attention to preventive efforts of this kind. Moreover, Kaplan shows that more flexibility in sentencing white collar criminals will go a long way toward correcting their behavior and discouraging others.

The University Community

One of the main themes of *Interactive Corporate Compliance* is the inadequacy of current legal and business education for preparing leaders who can participate in more cooperative relationships between business and government. In 1983 Dean Derek Bok of Harvard Law School (later president of Harvard University) told his startled audience that there were too many lawyers and too much litigation in America. He emphasized that legal training in the nation's law schools focused on adversarial skills and neglected training in reconciliation and accommodation. This legal training, he said, has added to the prevalence of conflict in American life. In our view this adversarial training has hampered the prospects for greater cooperation between business and government in favor of a more gladiatorial approach.

Professor Thomas L. Shaffer (together with Professor Robert S. Redmount) has made the most thorough survey of the subject by prying into the motivations and aspirations of law students. What they discovered reinforced Bok's essential point. Law schools are very similar all over the United States in that competition is a pervasive part of the atmosphere. This law school climate, Shaffer believes, sets the tone for the student's experiences in law school. The climate of law schools encourages aggressiveness and an adversary approach to resolving disputes.

So pervasive is the climate of American law schools that many students are converted by it to less altruistic attitudes. As many of the interviews suggest, students are much more concerned with justice in human affairs when entering law schools than when they leave as graduates. Apparently disillusionment is rampant among second- and third-year students, and competitiveness is enhanced by the climate of most law schools. Readers should consider these students' comments with care. They are poignant, graphic, and sometimes quite chilling.

As Shaffer points out, law schools have introduced some courses in human skills, such as counseling, but much more must be done to humanize the law school curriculum. He proposes some specific reforms to introduce a more humanistic climate. Until such reforms are instituted it appears likely that law schools will continue to produce gladiators, rather than mediators.

We believe that equating competition with litigation is one of the major weaknesses of legal education. Interactive compliance suggests a movement away from litigation and toward helping clients seek the rewards associated with being high compliers. The older values of legal education also ignore the value of promulgation because publication of the law (as opposed to winning lawsuits) is not a competitive value. If society gave incentives to and trained government agencies and their lawyers to communicate the law and its values, there would be much more compliance with the law because corporations could know exactly what was expected of them, instead of being forced to risk a competitive-style lawsuit.

For corporate counsel, interactive compliance has special significance. It requires a commitment to professional integrity, in addition to the obligation to serve the client. Corporate counsel may be called on to find a way to do something that the law or regulators forbid. The legal education of corporate counsel does not usually supply help in resolving this conflict, as some of the students' comments in Shaffer's chapter reveal. These problems of values and the amoral posture demanded by some corporate clients deserve attention at the law school level.

Law schools need to move toward the model of the counselor, and away from that of the legal gladiator. Given the trend of business and society to rely on complex organizations, lawyers need to understand the organizational nature and the group context of the modern corporation if they are to be effective, give good advice, and avoid frustrating the public interest.

W. Richard Sherman does not give good reports about business education either. Business students, too, are steeped in the competitive values of their curricula. Money still rules, and numbers have come to play a role almost as important as money itself. The pursuit of quantification is found in accounting, finance, and marketing courses, among many others, in which the "bottom line" is either money or some surrogate measure for money.

Sherman tells us that corporate compliance is not a regular part of the business curriculum. Some elements of compliance may be buried in vaguely titled courses concerning the legal environment of business. Even business ethics, a newly emerged field of instruction, proves a disappointment. While it is true that business ethics have been growing in significance, the field remains an orphan, outside the mainstream of business instruction, although mandated by professional societies. The entrepreneur who takes ethical shortcuts and cuts legal corners to win the competitive race still draws more sympathy from new business graduates than does the headquarters compliance "bureaucrat" who bars the road to a lucrative (but illegal) scheme.

Sherman also cautions us that business schools need to be persuaded to pay more attention to compliance as a subject. Cooperation with government is certainly not encouraged and the notion of possible government incentives for compliance is virtually inconceivable at present.

Sherman does tell us that the accounting model of interactive corporate compliance holds some hope for the future, given the prestige of the accounting profession and the experiences with the internal auditing function. In many other ways the accounting model might be the most familiar and least intrusive means of teaching, the techniques that will improve internal corporate control over undesired behavior. If so, courses in business ethics will probably not do as much to change the behavior and expectations of newly hatched businesspeople as will examples derived from the practices of accounting firms.

Sigler, in his chapter listing various government initiatives in interactive compliance, offers a key final step in meeting what John T. Scholz identifies as a crucial need for cooperative compliance efforts: political education. Scholz adds to this the requirement for enhanced regulatory resources to administer cooperative programs and suggests the creation of an institution to meet these needs: a National

Academy of Regulatory Enforcement. This fits our view of interactive compliance because this new academy could focus on precise methods to implement a cooperative strategy.

Scholz's call for enhanced regulatory resources may be a far more difficult proposal to sustain than the National Academy plan, given the present severe budget constraints, prevalent resistance to new taxation, and business reluctance to fund, through taxes, its historical adversary. At least a partial solution may rest in further explorations of the interactive compliance model. This model may permit leveraging of substantial compliance resources that are not funded through taxation.

A fully interactive compliance system would imaginatively utilize rewards and incentives for business and encourage competition among businesses to pursue those rewards. As with any other competitive approach, advantages to society would be derived from the challenges of producing a superior product—in this case a superior compliance control system. Successful businesses that reach the highest level of compliance could even find commercial value in their programs, licensing them, franchising them, and providing training and expertise to other businesses. Of course, the prize for which businesses would compete would be some form of government incentive or reward.

So we propose going beyond Scholz in delegating implementation of compliance programs to businesses as surrogates of government, with government still in a position to evaluate and monitor results. However, evaluation of implementation may not be solely the responsibility of either business or government. Other interested groups—industry experts, public interest groups and university centers, or even Scholz's National Academy—could serve as sources of suggested measurements for use in evaluations. Ultimately, though, someone would have to select a standard measure of performance, and this task may fall on government, after having heard proposals for alternative evaluation schemes.

Once relatively objective and acceptable measurement standards are set, compliance-oriented groups would have their tasks mapped for them. Such groups may be found inside corporations, as well as in government. Empowering such groups inside corporations to perform public compliance functions may be the most cost-effective technique for implementation of compliance programs. The OSHA Star Program, which empowers safety officers, union officials, and workers to report and correct safety problems, is the germ of such a concept.

However, Scholz has advanced this discussion by identifying political education as a major task that his National Academy would address.

An effective effort of this sort requires attention to different audiences and subgroups within corporations and within society if it is to work. We believe that the process of building greater cooperation between government and business must be gradual, not a wholesale assault on the public psyche, as Scholz seems to suggest. Our more gradualist approach would begin with the natural allies of interactive compliance: the groups and individuals within corporations who believe in the development of effective compliance programs and techniques. They can be found in most large organizations, but they must be encouraged and supported to supply the needs of the public, as Bezich has done in his experiment with the Camden County Silver Platter program.

We agree with Scholz that a national center or academy dealing with issues of regulatory compliance would lead to greater definition and legitimacy. Such a center could discover which techniques might lead to higher compliance. The center could look inside corporations to identify the various component units that could assist in compliance. It could help identify working compliance programs as models for certain industries. Most important, it could encourage government to experiment with alternative incentive systems for compliance purposes. The National Academy of Regulatory Enforcement has an impressive ring to its name. If it could gain public and industry acceptance, many of the adversary elements of regulatory behavior could be modified. Nonetheless, a great deal of spadework must be done before business, political groups, public interest groups, and other players in the regulatory arena could be satisfied as to the fairness, competence, and impartiality of the new entity. Nomenclature would have to be established, and a clear charter must be provided. The mandate of the new group would have to be defined so specifically that it does not give rise to new and more complex conflicts. We wonder whether sufficient agreement exists to launch such a venture. Meanwhile, we prefer more limited, empirical pilot programs in interactive compliance.

GOING FORWARD

The contributors have added vital, thought-provoking examples and analyses to the concepts of interactive compliance. In addition to their points, what are the future directions in this call for cooperative and results-oriented control of corporate conduct?

The point introduced by Attorney General Abrams deserves much more attention and analysis. Both John Braithwaite in his work on tripartism (1989) and Rutgers University Professor Richard Harris

(1991) have emphasized the critical roles of public interest groups in the development of society's relationship with corporations. These groups are unquestionably a dynamic force which must be reckoned with in all efforts at corporate control.

However, in finding a place for such groups one must also be careful not to oversimplify the complex nature of public interest analysis. Within the general framework of public interest are a variety of specific interests and a variety of perspectives. Thus, for example, labor and environmental groups may agree on decreasing workplace pollutants, but strongly disagree on development of new industrial facilities. Within the environmental movement there will be hawks who seek to punish industry and doves who seek workable compromises.

In interactive corporate compliance we would propose to refocus the hawks on those businesses that opt not to participate in cooperative systems. We would also expect public interest groups to help monitor corporate conduct to assure that those who have signed up for interactive programs are, in fact, faithful in these objectives. But we also propose to make public interest groups more effective in the same way that we believe government can become more effective: by adding positive elements to their arsenals. We do not believe it is necessary to restrict public interest groups to mere campaigns of reaction and hostility. We believe these groups have a very important role to play in rewarding positive corporate conduct and in offering ideas for and analysis on how to improve compliance efforts. Awareness of this potential can be seen in consumer advocate Ralph Nader's own willingness to recognize and publicly acknowledge socially responsive corporate conduct (*Business Week* 1989). We believe that if more effective empirical techniques are developed to demonstrate positive effects from voluntary compliance programs, this will reinforce all those who are interested in cooperative efforts, including those public interest groups that are concerned with achieving effective results. For example, if it can be shown that an interactive approach significantly reduces pollution among participants as compared to approaches that rely solely on the litigation process, this will appeal to all parties who are concerned with the environment.

An International Focus

Interactive Corporate Compliance (Sigler and Murphy 1988) was based on the writers' experiences in the United States. However, the work of Braithwaite and others shows that there are common concerns and a common need throughout the world. We believe there is much that Americans can learn from others about control of corporate conduct. Perhaps there are more cooperative models in certain areas of corporate conduct in other societies.

Similarly, there are certainly experiences in the American context that can be useful in other countries. While the United States has placed great emphasis on criminalization, it has also had much experience in developing in-house compliance techniques. American companies probably have more substantial in-house compliance groups, such as corporate counsel. It would be useful for their foreign counterparts to understand the role of American counsel, auditors, safety engineers, and similar groups. To the extent that the United States is willing to take a lead in developing interactive programs this nation can demonstrate how to use competition to enhance compliance efforts.

Understanding the Corporation

The success of interactive corporate compliance and indeed the success of any effort to control corporate conduct call for better definition and better understanding of the corporation. We see the existing lack of realism as a striking gap especially apparent in legal analysis.

Existing models of the corporation tend to be lifeless reflections of the real institutions. In the simplest analyses corporations are analogized to individual human beings. This makes further analysis relatively simple, but unfortunately also relatively meaningless. It is unrealistic to view an organization of tens of thousands of humans as if it were an individual person.

Only somewhat more advanced is the view of the corporation as a meeting point for 50,000 individuals, each making separate decisions as he or she works next to the others in the corporation. In this perspective each individual makes his or her own value judgments and perhaps would act the same way if working in isolation or in a different institution.

From the individualistic approaches flows the notion of management by conspiracy. In this view business is controlled by a board of directors or a group of executives who rationally weigh the legal risks and economic benefits of their decisions. In this view the allegations in the Pinto case are typical. Committee members weigh the cost of human death against profit to the shareholders and then determine by majority vote how many human lives are expendable. While this model makes wonderful newspaper copy and fits well with dry intellectual analysis, it is just as much fiction as the other stories that seem to attribute every other element of American history to conspiratorial groups.

Equally lifeless and devoid of reality is the legal theory that a corporation is merely a piece of property owned by its shareholders. While this makes sense in the context of two close friends forming a corporation and hiring a worker, it bears almost no relationship to multibillion dollar institutions employing hundreds of thousands of individuals and affecting millions of lives.

In this model there is a strict adherence to the view that the corporation is the shareholders' property and that its only reason for being is to generate profits for its owners. In fact, corporations today may often view share owners as merely a source of capital very much akin to bondholders. When the corporation needs capital, it decides, based on economic factors, whether to issue more stock or more debt. Anyone who has been in a corporation cannot help but notice the general irrelevance of share owners in the operation of the business. Of course, managers are concerned if a major event occurs with regard to the reaction of the share owners, but this is more the exception than the rule. It is hard to argue realistically that the shareholders have anything near the stake in a corporation that the employees or the suppliers or the customers have. Moreover, when the corporation is in financial trouble, its shareholders may even have less of a stake than the bondholders do. Thus, while it is intellectually easy to focus on the model of shareholders as the principal players, we view this as an analytical laziness that avoids the difficult work of understanding what corporations are actually about.

Interactive compliance does not ignore the legal framework of the corporation, but recognizes that this framework provides little guidance for controlling corporate conduct. Rather, we see the pluralistic model of American society as more in keeping with the dynamics of the corporation. This approach does not fit the tidy analytical models of the Chicago school or traditional legal analysis. Instead, we rely on the understanding of complex group interactions within the organization. We acknowledge the diffuse decision-making process in large institutions. Rather than attempting to fight against the reality of corporate organizations, we propose that society use those organizational dynamics for its own benefit. But neither we nor anyone else who attempts to deal with corporations can do so effectively without better analytical tools and better empirical understandings of these institutions. New insights are needed in order to deal most effectively with these entities.

There is a need for more empirical work to construct useful theories and models of the corporation. What is the role of groups within a corporation and how can they fit into the legal and economic models? For example, should the criminal justice system take into account departments and working groups within corporations? Should a working group suffer punishment? And how can the economic models be modified to explain the bakery example in Murphy's discussion of corporate compliance? Why would a $20 payment to every worker in a group be a more effective compliance method than the litigation risk of enormous economic loss for noncompliance?

There is a need for better legal and economic handles on the role of institutions within institutions. How can the role of law departments and auditors in corporations be better defined? And what additional professional guidance can be provided for the lawyers, auditors, and engineers? The existing legal analysis leads to such pointless results as advising corporate lawyers that they should resign if they disagree with proposed corporate misconduct. The end result is a loss to the lawyers, to the corporations, and to society. Certainly, legal scholarship can produce a better result than this.

Those concerned with corporate control also need better understanding and recognition of the role of corporate cultures. There is general acceptance in the literature that there is such a thing as a corporate culture and that those who attempt to implement compliance programs must take this into account (Deal and Kennedy 1982). However, attempts have not yet been made to weave this into economic or legal analysis. Perhaps if students of the corporation can develop useful empirical data on these points, this information can be used to mold the development of corporate criminal law and to help replace calcified legal theories that are no longer useful.

WHAT ARE THE NEXT PRACTICAL STEPS?

Interactive corporate compliance attempts to take a broad view of corporate conduct and methods to prevent corporate lawbreaking. However, this is an incremental approach that does not look for revolutionary change. Our objective is not to replace traditional approaches, but to supplement them with new thinking and new techniques. Our work is dedicated to a step-by-step transition in a number of related areas.

The development of effective corporate compliance techniques is a cornerstone for controlling corporate conduct. In the legal community we are supporting development of corporate compliance as a separately recognized specialty. We see a strong analogy to trial practice where a lawyer may have subject matter expertise in specific areas, but nevertheless be viewed as a "trial lawyer." We see in corporate compliance that certain techniques and skills are common to almost all compliance work. We see a need for practitioners in this area to develop these techniques and skills in a way similar to the development of trial skills and for law schools to include this as part of the training for new lawyers. In the same way that those schools have moot courts and trial practice they should also practice the techniques of preventive law involving business organizations. How is this transformation of the legal community to occur? We propose the development of workshops to focus on these techniques, modeled after similar efforts in trial practice. If these can be jointly sponsored by the bar and the law schools, that process will help introduce this area of practice to the schools. We also actively support the testing of new compliance techniques and the publication of information about those efforts, including the development of methods to test the results of these new techniques.

Perhaps a more controversial proposal is to revisit professional ethics for lawyers to address the duty of the professional within a corporate institution. We believe that the rules that apply to lawyers representing individual clients are outmoded in this context. For example, the question should be carefully examined whether a lawyer's duty goes beyond merely providing legal advice when requested by the client and demands a more active role in preventing violations within the corporation and in helping to manage the compliance process. If the legal profession is charged with a responsibility to society, then perhaps it is time to recognize the unique role of counsel within corporate organizations. Rather than advising lawyers that they should resign from representing their client when they believe their corporate client's activity is illegal, more thought should be given to requiring lawyers to escalate these concerns within the institution. Perhaps a lawyer who suspects wrongdoing should be obliged or at least have the option professionally to escalate his or her concerns within the institution to the board of directors and perhaps, in extreme cases, to the shareholders. Accompanying this authority would be protection from wrongful discharge by the company. We do not purport to have the answers to these questions, but we do believe that these questions should be examined without the hindrance of outdated models of the corporate client.

In order to effect even incremental changes it is necessary to develop consensus among those concerned with corporate conduct. One important step is to bring together those who support business ethics and those who are devoted to corporate compliance. We need to communicate to the ethicists that those who support corporate compliance do, in fact, have a broader, value-oriented perspective, although this is not reflected in their institutional vocabulary. While they speak in terms of compliance with laws and rules, their impact on corporations is, in fact, to increase the value-sensitivity of those institutions. On the other side of the balance, it is necessary to communicate to those involved in corporate compliance the fact that many business ethicists are interested in finding effective techniques to influence corporate conduct. These efforts will in turn help mold corporate cultures so that they are conducive to effective compliance techniques.

We offer to both the business ethicists and the corporate compliance advocates the challenge to start measuring the results of their respective efforts. As long as debate is limited to intuitive arguments and conceptual issues, there will be little progress. If, however, all participants are required to demonstrate the actual results of their respective positions, it may be possible to replace aimless debate with actual progress.

At the same time that many within the corporate world are responding to the challenge to develop new techniques one must also be cognizant of the risks associated with existing litigation systems. In order to minimize this serious distraction we are pushing strongly for development of doctrines within the legal system to protect internal compliance efforts. The most important step here would be further development and enhancement of the self-evaluative privilege. We propose that ongoing internal compliance reviews be protected from discovery and use in the litigation process. In fact, we propose more than the traditional privilege; we support legal immunity for good faith compliance audits. Except where compliance efforts are shams, used to enhance criminal conduct, we believe that the legal process should bar all use of such efforts against corporations. Traditional privilege issues, such as waiver of the privilege, should be viewed as irrelevant. The issue is not the confidentiality of such internal compliance efforts. In fact, effective compliance efforts may require substantial publicity within the corporation in order to make them effective. The public policy value is not merely to protect confidentiality, but rather to promote the underlying conduct as a value in itself. Effective corporate compliance activities need to be viewed as an alternative method to litigation to promote corporate compliance.

Such a change in legal thinking will not be brought about quickly. However, merely promoting debate in this area will help to sharpen the focus on the issues. If it helps the future judges, legislators, prosecutors, and corporate counsel to better understand the crucial nature of corporate internal compliance activities and the need for society to promote those activities, then the debate itself will have a lasting, long-term benefit.

Interactive compliance seeks more than mere tolerance by the government. It also calls for active government support and promotion of voluntary corporate efforts. As the chapters by Bezich and Sigler indicate, a few nascent programs are starting to create an environment in which such programs can grow. There is a basic need for government to better understand the nature of corporate compliance. There may be great value in having government representatives participate in the symposia and conferences provided for corporate counsel and other constituencies that deal with compliance efforts so that government may see firsthand how seriously this is viewed in private enterprise. Corporate managers cannot expect government to accept on faith the importance of such compliance efforts. Rather, managers should provide as much information and background as possible so that agency administrators, legislators, and prosecutors can understand the complexity, resource allocations, and degree of devotion required for effective compliance programs.

Much can be gained from promoting the use of incentives or "carrots" by government agencies. Experience indicates that the most likely starting point is for government to offer favorable publicity for those organizations that take the lead in compliance efforts. Beyond this there are the proposals for limitations on penalties such as those described in the Pitt-Groskaufmanis chapter. There are numerous other possibilities such as providing cash awards or special government liaison officers for high-complying companies.

In summary, then, we see numerous arenas where progress can be made. Of critical importance throughout all these efforts, however, is the need to bring together those who have common experiences in order to share their ideas and knowledge. We should begin by recognizing that while there are many different schools of thought and modes of expression in this area, there is a fairly large community of interest among those who seek to improve corporate conduct.

The April 1990 conference at New York University was a first major step in this direction, bringing together, as it did, representatives of government, business, and the academic community. There is a clear value in continuing such conferences.

We also propose to initiate an ongoing publication to maintain communications among those who believe in this common approach and common objective. We envision a business conduct newsletter addressed to this growing audience. It will report on practical, management-oriented approaches to compliance, providing insight on new techniques in the use of corporate incentives and controls. It will also include reports on practical ethics programs that are able to produce discernable results. In this publication we will provide ongoing news of government efforts to cooperate with and provide incentives for voluntary compliance. Reports will also be included on pragmatic, realistic university efforts to support these developments, including new teaching methods and new ways to measure the results of compliance programs.

We do not, then, see a quick, dramatic shift from litigation to cooperation. On the other hand, we do believe that enough people will see the futility of sole reliance on criminal enforcement and litigation. We do not believe society's choices are limited to regulation or deregulation. While that debate will, of course, continue, we believe that an interactive approach will become an increasingly valuable alternative in the 1990s.

References

Ackerman, Robert. 1973. How Companies Respond to Social Demands. *Harvard Business Review* 51 (no. 4): 88–98.

Advertising Age. 1989. Consumers Go Green. 60 (no. 3): 92.

Allen, Ronald J., and Cynthia M. Hazelwood. 1987. Preserving the Confidentiality of Internal Corporate Investigations. *Journal of Corporation Law* 12: 355–81.

American Assembly of Collegiate Schools of Business. 1989. *Accreditation Council Policies, Procedures, and Standards. 1989–90*. St. Louis, MO.

American Law Institute. 1985. *Model Penal Code*. Philadelphia: American Law Institute.

Axelrod, Robert. 1984. *The Evolution of Cooperation*. New York: Basic Books.

Ayers, Ian, and John Braithwaite. 1989. Tripartism, Empowerment, and Game-theoretic Notions of Regulatory Capture. Paper presented at the Law and Society Association meeting, June, Madison, Wisconsin.

Bardach, Eugene, and Robert A. Kagan. 1982. *Going by the Book: The Problem of Regulatory Unreasonableness*. Philadelphia: Temple University Press.

Beggs, Joyce M., and Michael S. Lane. 1989. Corporate Goal Structure and Business Students: A Comparative Study of Values. *Journal of Business Ethics* 8 (no. 6): 471–78.

Bok, Derek. 1983. A Flawed System of Law Practice and Training. *Journal of Legal Education* 33: 570–585.

Braithwaite, John. 1982. Enforced Self-Regulation: A New Strategy for Corporate Crime Control. *Michigan Law Review* 80: 1466–1507.

———. 1985a. *To Punish or Persuade: Enforcement of Coal Mine Safety.* Albany: State University of New York Press.

———. 1985b. Taking Responsibility Seriously: Corporate Compliance Systems. In *Corrigible Corporations and Unruly Law*, ed. Brent Fisse and Peter A. French, 39–61. San Antonio: Trinity University Press.

Brown, Louis M., and Anne O. Kandel. 1990. *The Legal Audit: Corporate Internal Investigation.* New York: Clark Boardman Co.

Business Conference Board. 1987. *Corporate Ethics.* New York: The Conference Board.

———. 1990. *Corporate Ethics.* New York: The Conference Board.

Business Week. 1989. The Second Coming of Ralph Nader (6 March): 28.

Byrne, J. A., and A. Beam. 1987. Harvard's $30 Million Windfall for Ethics 101. *Business Week* (13 April 1987): 40.

Center for Business Ethics. 1986. Are Corporations Institutionalizing Ethics? *Journal of Business Ethics* 5 (April): 87–88.

Coffee, John C., Jr. 1981. "No Soul to Damn: No Body to Kick": An Unscandalized Inquiry Into the Problem of Corporate Punishment. *Michigan Law Review* 79: 386–459.

———. 1990. For Some Companies, Supervision Is the Best Form of Punishment. *Legal Times* 23 (19 Feb.): 2.

Comegys, Walker B. 1986. *Antitrust Compliance Manual: A Guide for Counsel, Management, and Public Officials.* New York: Practicing Law Institute.

Cressy, Donald R., and Charles A. Moore. 1983. Managerial Values and Corporate Codes of Ethics. *California Management Review* 25: 69–71.

Cutler, Robert. 1983. Environmental Auditing: The Keystone to a Management Compliance, Control and Risk Assessment Program. In *Sixth Annual Institute for Corporate Counsel*, 13–26. New York: Practicing Law Institute.

Deal, Terrence E., and Allen A. Kennedy. 1982. *Corporate Cultures: The Rites and Rituals of Corporate Life.* Reading, Mass.: Addison-Wesley.

Demaris, Ovid. 1964. *Dirty Business: The Corporate-Political-Money-Power-Game.* New York: Avon Books.

DiMento, Joseph D. 1986. *Environmental Law and American Business.* New York: Plenum Press.

Dunfee, Thomas W. 1986. *Integrating Ethics into the MBA Curriculum.* Philadelphia: Wharton School of the University of Pennsylvania.

———. 1987. The Case for Professional Norms of Business Ethics. *American Business Law Journal* 25 (no. 3): 385–406.

Ethics Resource Center. 1984. *Survey of Ethics Codes*: Washington, D.C.: ERC.

———. 1987. *It's Up to You: A Management Accountant's Decisions.* Washington, D.C.: ERC. Videotape.

Frank, Nancy, and Michael Lombness. 1988. Gaining Regulatory Compliance. *Administration and Society* 20: 71–91.

Frederick, William C. 1983. Corporate Social Responsibility in the Reagan Era and Beyond. *California Management Review* 25: 145–57.

———. 1987. *Research in Corporate Social Performance and Social Policy: Empirical Studies of Business Ethics and Values.* Greenwich, Conn.: JAI Press.

Freeman, R. Edward, and Daniel R. Gilbert, Jr. 1988. *Corporate Strategy and the Search for Ethics.* Englewood Cliffs, N.J.: Prentice-Hall.

Fried, Frank, Harris, Shriver and Jacobson. 1984. 1987. Surveys of Corporate Codes of Conduct. *Georgetown Law Journal* on file.

Garrett, James J. 1978. *Antitrust Compliance: A Legal and Business Guide.* New York: Practicing Law Institute.

Goffman, Erving. 1959. *The Presentation of the Self in Everyday Life.* New York: Doubleday.

Goldblatt, Michael. 1989. *Preventive Law in Corporate Practice.* New York: Matthew Bender.

Graetz, Micheal J., Jennifer F. Reinganum, and Louis J. Wilde. 1986. The Tax Compliance Game: Toward an Interactive Theory of Law Enforcement. *Journal of Law, Economics and Organization* 2: 1–32

Greenberg, Joseph. 1984. Avoiding Tax Avoidance: A (repeated) Game-theoretic Approach. *Journal of Economic Theory* 32: 1–13.

Harris, Richard A. 1991. *Government, Business, and the New Politics of Regulation.* Baltimore, Md.: Johns Hopkins.

Hawkins, Keith and John M. Thomas. 1984. *Enforcing Regulation.* Boston: Kluwer-Nijhoff.

Homer, LaRue T., and Nicholas H. Stenek. 1989. Teaching Business Ethics: The Use of Films and Videotape. *Journal of Business Ethics* 8 (no. 12): 929–36.

Huber, Peter. 1988. *Liability: The Legal Revolution and Its Consequences.* New York: Basic Books.

Josephson, Michael. 1989. Easier Said Than Done. *Ethics* 1 (March 1989): 70–72.

Kagan, Robert. A. 1978. *Regulatory Justice: Implementing a Wage-Price Freeze.* New York: Russell Sage Foundation.

Kagan, Robert A., and John T. Scholz. 1984. The "Criminology" of the Corporation and Regulatory Enforcement Strategies. In *Enforcing Regulation,* ed. Keith Hawkins and John M. Thomas, (pp. 380–421). Boston: Kluwer-Nijhoff.

Kaplan, Jeffrey M. 1988. Making the Most of Sentencing. *National Law Journal* (22 Feb.): 3.

Kelman, Steven. 1982. *Regulating America. Regulating Sweden.* Cambridge: MIT Press.

King, Mervyn N. 1977. *Public Policy and the Corporation.* New York: Wiley.

Lane, Michael S., and Dietrich Schaupp. 1989. Ethics in Education: A Comparative Study. *Journal of Business Ethics* 8: 943–49.

Leary, Thomas B. 1977. Suggestions for an Effective Compliance Program from the Perspective of Corporate Counsel. *Antitrust Law Journal* 46: 490–96.

Leavitt, Harold J. 1989. Educating our MBAs: On Teaching What We Haven't Taught. *California Management Review* 31: 38–50.

Leonard, David P. 1988. Codifying a Privilege for Self-Critical Analysis. *Harvard Journal on Legislation* 12: 355–81.

Lipson, Barry J. 1971. How to Implement an Antitrust Compliance Program. *Practical Lawyer* 17: 39–44.

Luthy, Richard F., Jr. 1989. Fairfield-Suisin Sewer District. LOGIN Database: T84793.

Marcus, Alfred. 1984. *The Adversary Economy.* Westport, Conn.: Quorum Books.

Mathews, M. Cash. *Strategic Intervention in Organizations.* 1988. Newbury Park, Calif.: Sage.

Miller, Samuel R., and Lawrence C. Levine. 1984. Recent Developments in Corporate Criminal Liability. *Santa Clara Law Review* 24: 46–56.

Mitnick, Barry. 1980. Incentive Systems in Environmental Regulation. *Policy Studies Journal* 9: 379–92.

Mitnick, Barry, R. W. Backoff, and H. G. Rainey. 1977. The Incentive System Approach to the Study of Public Organizations. Paper presented at the annual meeting of the American Political Science Association, Washington, D.C.

Mokhiber, Russell. 1988. *Corporate Crime and Violence: Big Business Power and the Abuse of the Public Trust.* San Francisco: Sierra Club Books.

Muir, William K. 1977. *Police: Streetcorner Politicians.* Chicago: University of Chicago Press.

Nader, Ralph J., Mark Green, and Joel Seligman. 1976. *Taming the Giant Corporation.* New York: W. W. Norton.

National Journal. 1986. Resolving Disputes. (15 Nov.): 2764.

Newsweek. 1990. Solving Problems. (27 Aug.): 48.

Nonet, Phillipe, and Phillip Selznick. 1978. *Law and Society in Transition: Toward Responsive Law.* New York: Harper Colophon Books.

Olson, Mancur. 1965. *The Logic of Collective Action.* Cambridge: Harvard University Press.

Opinion Research Corporation. 1980. *Implementation and Enforcement of Codes of Ethics in Corporations and Associations.* Princeton, N.J.: Opinion Research Corporation.

Pitt, Harvey L., and Karl A. Groskaufmanis. 1990. Minimizing Corporate Civil and Criminal Liability: A Second Look at Corporate Codes of Conduct. *Georgetown Law Journal* 78: 1559–654.

President's Blue Ribbon Commission on Defense Management. *A Quest for Excellence: Final Report to the President, 1986.* Washington, D.C.: The Commission.

Preston, Lee, and James Post. 1975. *Private Management and Public Policy.* Englewood Cliffs, N.J.: Prentice-Hall.

Reinganum, Jennifer F. and Louis J. Wilde. 1986. Equilibrium Verification and Reporting Policies in a Model of Tax Compliance. *International Economics Review* 27: 739–60.

Report of the National Commission on Fraudulent Financial Reporting. 1987. Washington, D.C.: Government Printing Office.

Richardson, Margaret. 1986. How Exceeding Compliance Benefits Government. Speech delivered at Hazmet West, 4 Dec., Los Angeles.

Rogers, Carl. 1972. *On Becoming a Person.* Boston: Houghton Mifflin.

Scholz, John T. 1984a. Cooperation, Deterrence, and the Ecology of Regulatory Enforcement. *Law and Society Review* 18: 601–46.

———. 1984b. Voluntary Compliance and Regulatory Enforcement. *Law and Policy* 6: 385–404.

———. 1984c. Reliability, Responsiveness, and Regulatory Policy. *Public Administration Review* 44 (April): 145–53.

———. 1989. Federal vs. State Regulation: Does It Matter? In *Power Divided: Essays on the Theory and Practice of Federalism*, ed. Malcolm Feeley and Harry Scheiber, 221–245. Berkeley, Calif.: Institute of Governmental Studies.

Shaffer, Thomas L. and Robert S. Redmount. 1977. *Lawyers, Law Students and People*. Colorado Springs: Shepard's.

Shover, Neil, John Lynxwiler, and Donald Clelland. 1983. *Developing a Regulatory Bureaucracy: The Office of Surface Mining Reclamation and Enforcement*. Washington, D.C.: National Institute of Justice.

Sigler, Jay A., and Joseph E. Murphy. 1988. *Interactive Corporate Compliance: An Alternative to Regulatory Compulsion*. Westport, Conn.: Greenwood Press.

Silbey, Susan. 1984. The Consequences of Responsive Regulation. In *Enforcing Regulation*. ed. Keith Hawkins and John Thomas, 145–68. Boston: Kluwer-Nijhoff.

Silverstein, David. 1987. Managing Corporate Social Responsibility in a Changing Legal Environment. *American Business Law Journal* 25: 523–66.

Southwestern School of Banking. 1980. *A Study of Corporate Ethical Policy Statements*. Dallas: Southern Methodist University Press.

Stanton, Ann L. 1986. *Florida's Model Energy Efficiency Code for Building Construction*. Tallahassee, Fla.: State Housing Office. Mimeo.

Stone, Christopher. 1975. *Where the Law Ends: The Social Control of Corporate Behavior*. New York: Harper & Row.

———. 1981. Corporations and Law at the Pass: Towards a General Theory of Compliance Strategy. *Wisconsin Law Review* 1981: 861–90.

Thornburgh, Richard. 1990. U.S. Government Is Going After the Savings and Loan Cheats. *Philadelphia Inquirer* 2 Sept., F7.

Time. 1989. A Stinking Mess. (2 Jan.): 45.

United States Sentencing Commission. 1989. Notice of Proposed Additions to Sentencing Guidelines, Policy Statements and Commentary. Request for Public Comment. *BNA Antitrust and Trade Regulation Report* (9 Nov.): 663–70.

Webb, Margaret K. 1990. At Ottenberg's, a Recipe for Rewarding Safety. *Washington Post*, 19 Feb., F11.

White, Bernard J. 1980. Corporate Codes of Conduct: A Mechanism of Internal Control. In *Internal Control in American Corporations: The State of the Art*, ed. Robert K. Mautz, 381–90. New York: Financial Executives Research Foundation.

Whiting, Richard A. 1962. Antitrust and the Corporate Executive II. *University of Virginia Law Review* 48: 1–49.

Table of Cases

Atasi Corp. v. Seagate Technology, 847 F.2d 826 (Fed. Cir. 1988).

Cotton v. Merrill Lynch, Pierce, Fenner & Smith, Inc., 699 F. Supp. 251 (N.D. Okla. 1988).

Harnischfager Corp. v. Paccar, 474 F. Supp. 1151 (E.D. Wis. 1979).

Kesselhaut v. United States, 555 F.2d 791 (Ct. Cl. 1977).

Kopper's Co. v. American Express Co., 689 F. Supp. 1371 (W.D. Pa. 1988).

LaSalle National Bank v. County of Lake, 703 F.2d 252 (7th Cir. 1983).

United States v. Allegheny Bottling Co., 695 F. Supp. 856 (E.D. Va. 1988), *reversed in part*, 870 F.2d 655 (4th Cir.), *cert. denied*, 110 S. Ct. 68 (1989).

United States v. Basic Construction Co., 711 F.2d 570 (5th Cir. 1983).

United States v. Beusch, 596 F.2d 871 (9th Cir. 1979).

Washington Steel Corp. v. TW Corp., 602 F.2d 594 (3rd Cir. 1979).

Yates v. Avco Corp., 819 F.2d 630 (6th Cir. 1987).

Index

About the Contributors

ROBERT ABRAMS is Attorney General of the state of New York, a position he has held since 1979. He was a member of the New York State Assembly from 1965 to 1969 and served as president of the Borough of the Bronx, New York City, in 1978. Attorney General Abrams has long been active in environmental law and antitrust matters.

LOUIS S. BEZICH is county administrator and treasurer, Camden County, New Jersey. From 1985 to 1987 he served as business administrator and treasurer of Washington Township, New Jersey. Mr. Bezich has taught public administration at Rutgers University and Glassboro State College. He is also active in various professional organizations.

JOHN BRAITHWAITE is a professor in the Research School for Social Sciences at the Australian National University. Professor Braithwaite has written extensively about problems in regulatory enforcement in Australia, the United States, the United Kingdom, and elsewhere. Perhaps his best-known books are *To Punish or Persuade* and *Of Manners Gentle*. In addition to his formidable scholarship, Professor Braithwaite has practical working experience with regulatory agencies in Australia and has helped in the construction of regulatory reform measures in that nation and in others. Currently, Professor Braithwaite is doing cross-cultural research on nursing home administration and regulation.

PAUL M. CARREN is the partner in charge of KPMG Peat Marwick's Government Contractor Advisory Services Group. He has worked extensively with government contractors in virtually every aspect of the contracting process, including contract compliance reviews, self-governance programs, and internal control reviews.

KARL A. GROSKAUFMANIS is an associate at Fried, Frank, Harris, Shriver & Jacobson in Washington, D.C., and a member of the Massachusetts and District of Columbia bars.

JEFFREY M. KAPLAN is a director of the nonprofit Business Ethics Study Team, Incorporated, and a member of the New York–based law firm of Chadbourne and Parke. He specializes in business crime–related litigation and internal investigations. Mr. Kaplan is the coauthor of *The Prevention and Prosecution of Computer and High Technology Crime* (1988) and the author of various articles on business crime.

JOSEPH E. MURPHY is a senior attorney with Bell Atlantic Corporation in Philadelphia and a member of the Pennsylvania and New Jersey bars. He is active in bar association activities to enhance corporate compliance and has published numerous articles on the subject. He is coauthor, with Jay A. Sigler, of *Interactive Corporate Compliance* (Greenwood Press, 1988) and is on the Business Ethics Study Team's advisory board.

RICHARD B. PAZORNIK is a senior consultant in the Government Contract Advisory Services Group with KPMG Peat Marwick in the company's Washington, D.C., office. Prior to joining KPMG Peat Marwick, Mr. Pazornik engaged in the private practice of law. He has also worked as senior contract administrator with the Bendix Communications Division of Allied-Signal, Inc.

HARVEY L. PITT is a partner at Fried, Frank, Harris, Shriver & Jacobson in Washington, D.C. Mr. Pitt previously held various positions with the Securities and Exchange Commission, including serving as general counsel to the commission. He is a frequent speaker and author of articles on federal securities and banking law issues and is also adjunct professor of law at The National Law Center at The George Washington University.

JOHN T. SCHOLZ is an associate professor of political science at the State University of New York, Stony Brook. He has worked on a variety of enforcement and compliance issues for the past decade. Dr. Scholz has published numerous articles and book chapters on these subjects. His two-volume book *Taxpayer Compliance*, written in collaboration with Jeffrey Roth and Anne Witte, was published in 1989.

THOMAS L. SHAFFER is Robert and Marion Short Professor of Law at Notre Dame Law School. He was dean of the Notre Dame Law School from 1971 to 1975. He is the author of many noteworthy books, including *Death, Property, and Lawyers* (1970), *On Being a Christian and a Lawyer* (1981), and *American Legal Ethics* (1985). The chapter presented here draws on the research collected by Professors Shaffer and Robert S. Redmount in *Lawyers, Law Students, and People* (1976).

W. RICHARD SHERMAN is both a lawyer and a CPA. He is an assistant professor of accounting at St. Joseph's University in Philadelphia. The recipient of several awards for teaching excellence, Professor Sherman has published articles in the *Accounting Historian's Journal, Journal of Accounting Education, Accounting Educator's Journal*, and *National Public Accountant*. Professor Sherman is a member of the American Accounting Association, the American Business Law Association, and the International Association for Accounting Education and Research, among other professional groups.

JAY A. SIGLER is chairman of the Graduate Department of Public Policy and Administration at Rutgers University. He is the author of fifteen books, including *Interactive Corporate Compliance*, coauthored with Joseph E. Murphy and published by Greenwood Press in 1988. Dr. Sigler has worked with the Environmental Protection Agency and has served as a consultant to the National Park Service and the Attorney General of the state of New Jersey, among others.

www.ingramcontent.com/pod-product-compliance
Ingram Content Group UK Ltd.
Pitfield, Milton Keynes, MK11 3LW, UK
UKHW020814290926
15470UKWH00003B/1145